T0195720

Global Innovation

Ned Hamson and Robert Holder

■ Fast track route to mastering global innovation

■ Covers the key areas of global innovation, from understanding what drives innovation in every area of your business to strategies for developing your own practical innovation management process

■ Examples and lessons from some of the world's most successful businesses, including Toyota, Nokia, QVC and Canon, and ideas from the smartest thinkers, including Joel Barker, Edward deBono, Harrison Owen, Ikujiro Nonaka, Hidaki Yoshihara, Richard Branson and Linus Torvalds

■ Includes a glossary of key concepts and a comprehensive resources guide

>>EXPRESS EXEC.COM<<
essential management thinking at your fingertips

First published 2002 by
Capstone Publishing (a Wiley company)
8 Newtec Place
Magdalen Road
Oxford OX4 1RE
United Kingdom
http://www.capstoneideas.com

CIP catalogue records for this book are available from the British Library and the US Library of Congress

ISBN 1-84112-219-X

This book is printed on acid-free paper

Substantial discounts on bulk quantities of Capstone books are available to corporations, professional associations and other organizations. Please contact Capstone for more details on +44 (0)1865 798 623 or (fax) +44 (0)1865 240 941 or (e-mail) info@wiley-capstone.co.uk

Contents

Introduction to

ExpressExec

ExpressExec is 3 million words of the latest management thinking compiled into 10 modules. Each module contains 10 individual titles forming a comprehensive resource of current business practice written by leading practitioners in their field. From brand management to balanced scorecard, ExpressExec enables you to grasp the key concepts behind each subject and implement the theory immediately. Each of the 100 titles is available in print and electronic formats.

Through the ExpressExec.com Website you will discover that you can access the complete resource in a number of ways:

» printed books or e-books;
» e-content – PDF or XML (for licensed syndication) adding value to an intranet or Internet site;
» a corporate e-learning/knowledge management solution providing a cost-effective platform for developing skills and sharing knowledge within an organization;
» bespoke delivery – tailored solutions to solve your need.

Why not visit www.expressexec.com and register for free key management briefings, a monthly newsletter and interactive skills checklists. Share your ideas about ExpressExec and your thoughts about business today.

Please contact elound@wiley-capstone.co.uk for more information.

Introduction to Global Innovation

» Why is global innovation an important topic for leaders and managers today?
» What is the Global Compact and what is its impact on global innovation?
» Global innovation today is not just innovation writ large and world-wide, it is changed and it will change how you do business and innovate.

Today, the choices open for global innovation are ever-expanding – so much so that it must be considered a new era for business and organizational innovation in general. One might call it global innovation plus. Why global innovation plus? Because a significant advance in technology or service is insufficient to make a mark today. There are additional concerns and issues that are now part and parcel of the global innovation process.

The following three items will illustrate for those who might doubt that we have entered a new era of global innovation, or wonder whether the changes are important or fundamental to their business.

"A little more than a year ago, we entered a five-year partnership called the Global Alliance for Workers and Communities. We're finding out directly from workers about their issues and needs and investing in programs to improve their work and life experience while in our contract factories.

"I believe the Global Alliance is an example of what we hope the Global Compact will inspire – cooperation among international and local companies, NGOs, and other organizations to address the impact of globalization with real solutions. We know from experience that these partnerships can work.

"The Global Alliance will operate in four countries its first two years, involve more than 30 factories, and about 170,000 workers, or a third of Nike's global contract factory workforce."

Philip H. Knight, chairman and CEO of Nike[1]

The World Wide Web Consortium (W3C):

"defines the Web as the universe of network-accessible information (available through your computer, phone, television, or networked refrigerator . . .). Today this universe benefits society by enabling new forms of human communication and opportunities to share knowledge. One of W3C's primary goals is to make these benefits available to all people, whatever their hardware, software, network infrastructure, native language, culture, geographical location, or physical or mental ability. W3C's Internationalization Activity, Device Independence Activity, Voice Browser Activity, and Web Accessibility Initiative all illustrate our commitment to universal access."

Statement at http://www.w3.org.

September 11, 2001: Terrorists hijack four commercial airliners in the US and three of them are intentionally crashed into occupied buildings (the World Trade Towers in New York and the Pentagon in Washington, DC) resulting in the deaths of thousands, as well as thousands injured but not killed.[2]

WHAT IS THE GLOBAL COMPACT AND WHAT IS ITS IMPACT ON GLOBAL INNOVATION?

Here is a concise statement on what the Global Compact is, drawn from the United Nation's Website:

"The Global Compact is not a regulatory instrument or code of conduct, but a value-based platform designed to promote institutional learning. It utilizes the power of transparency and dialogue to identify and disseminate good practices based on universal principles.

"The Compact encompasses nine such principles, drawn from the Universal Declaration of Human Rights, the ILO's [International Labour Organization] Fundamental Principles on Rights at Work, and the Rio Principles on Environment and Development ... And it asks companies to act on these principles in their own corporate domains. Thus, the Compact promotes good practices by corporations; it does not endorse companies."

"So," you say, "it's not law, so I don't need to worry about it." Those of you familiar with the growth in registrations for quality management to

ISO 9000–2000 standards and environmental standards to ISO 14000, know that once a significant number of big players "sign on" to a set of principles or standards, they are on their way to becoming a part of the business process.

During the operational phase, the Global Compact "was launched at a high-level event at UN Headquarters on 26 July 2000. The meeting, chaired by the Secretary-General, brought together senior executives from some 50 major corporations and the leaders of labor, human rights, environmental and development organizations."[3]

At this meeting, the chairman and CEO of Nike, Philip Knight, said:

"an internationally recognized set of generally accepted social accounting principles and monitoring organizations *certified* to measure performance would bring greater clarity to the impact of globalization and the performance of any one company."

Philip H. Knight[4]

We added emphasis to the word *certified* to show that, even at this early date, an industry giant, Nike, would prefer that the Global Compact resembles something like the ISO standards, as that would "level" the playing field – meaning that everyone would have to meet the same standards in standard operations as they innovate for the global market.

THE NINE PRINCIPLES OF THE GLOBAL COMPACT

1 The Secretary-General asked world business to support and respect the protection of internationally proclaimed human rights within their sphere of influence.
2 The Secretary-General asked world business to make sure they are not complicit in human rights abuses.
3 The Secretary-General asked world business to uphold freedom of association and effective recognition of the right to collective bargaining.
4 The Secretary-General asked world business to promote the elimination of all forms of forced and compulsory labor.

5 The Secretary-General asked world business to promote the effective abolition of child labor.

6 The Secretary-General asked world business to uphold the elimination of discrimination in respect of employment and occupation.

7 The Secretary-General asked world business to support a precautionary approach to environmental challenges.

8 The Secretary-General asked world business to undertake initiatives to promote greater environmental responsibility.

9 The Secretary-General asked world business to encourage the development and diffusion of environmentally friendly technologies.[5]

Take a look at the nine principles of the Global Compact (above) and the two examples of how relatively small players (below) in the global innovation game are working at becoming "players."

Think about the impact that the September 11 horror and innovation had on military, police, fire, and foreign policy planners' "paradigms" on innovation.

GLOBAL INNOVATION TODAY IS NOT JUST INNOVATION WRIT LARGE AND WORLDWIDE, IT IS CHANGED AND IT WILL CHANGE HOW YOU DO BUSINESS AND INNOVATE

Two small cities playing the global innovation game

Tomakomai City has a population of 175,000 and is located in Hokkaido, the most northerly, large, Japanese island. Its university is a branch of Komazawa University.

Tomakomai Komazawa University's Department of International Culture notes that:

> "... Tomakomai Komazawa University is affiliated with the University of Exeter in the United Kingdom of Great Britain, Dongguk University in Korea, the University of Queensland and Griffith University in Australia, the University of British Columbia in Canada, Arkansas Tech University, California State University at Los Angeles, University of California at Irvine, and the University of Hawaii at Manoa in the United States."

> The Borough of Rochdale is a small metropolitan borough in northwest England, not far from Manchester, a major industrial city for 200 years or more. In promoting itself, the business council notes that:

> > "Travel to Manchester International Airport takes about 35 minutes by road. The airport is the fastest growing in the UK, with daily flights to North America and the Far East, as well as scheduled services to every major European city."

So, why should you read this book on global innovation? We will write about global innovation taking those "innovation plus" issues into account wherever appropriate.

In addition, we offer views, experiences, tips, and examples based on our working knowledge of more than 1000 authors and companies from around the world and our experiences with more than 1000 companies over the past 15 years. Ned Hamson alone has worked with more than 1000 authors (people in organizations as well as consultants and researchers) and Bob Holder has viewed the work and experience of that many, at least, in his 15-plus years of interviewing, researching, and writing dozens of articles on innovation, change management, and discontinuous and continuous improvement.

This joint experience gives us a bias toward finding the most practical processes and methods that will fit the needs of organizations that want to create and/or sustain an effective and efficient approach to global innovation.

This means that instead of exhausting you, the reader, with all possible answers and resources, we will, to the best of our ability and experience, cut through the massive information glut on innovation and give you a practical and concise innovative book on global innovation.

NOTES

1 Knight was speaking at the United Nations in New York (July 26, 2000).

2 Authors' note: We know it is gruesome, but this attack is a terrible and significant example of global innovation in the methods of terror. It demonstrated that a group without an industrial base could accomplish the same amount of destruction as cruise missiles, which require significant industrial, technological, financial, political, and military sectors to construct and deliver.

3 Source: http://www.unglobalcompact.org/un/gc/unweb.nsf/content/WhatItIs.htm.

4 Source: http://www.nikebiz.com/media/n_compact.shtml.

5 For a detailed explanation of these principles, see http://www.unglobalcompact.org/.

What is Global Innovation?

» What is meant by global innovation?
» Scouting the future and scouting your way to success.
» "What's new?" has more than one meaning!
» The drivers of innovation.

First let's just look at innovation. As a term, it has been so overused in claims of many different types that some may view it as being as jaded as "new and improved."

Discontinuous innovation

Our take on innovation is in line with that of Professor Hidaki Yoshihara of Kobe University in Japan. His definition: "What is innovation? Briefly, innovation means denying existing conditions, or changing the existing order of things, or values, or systems." When we have written about it in the past, we have also called it discontinuous innovation.

Discontinuous innovation is the reconceptualizing of a product or service in one or more of four ways.

1 It makes doing something much, much easier.
   » It combines several tasks/functions into one operation.
   » It enables you to do something that could not be done by an individual prior to its introduction.
2 It greatly speeds up some processes.
3 It is a redefinition of beauty/style/feel/sensuality that makes the product or service much more enjoyable.
4 It greatly reduces cost while not sacrificing quality.

In short, continuity with the past is broken – seemingly forever and at once:

» Federal Express reinvented small parcel delivery;
» in the 1980s, the fax reinvented letter and memo delivery by destroying time;
» e-mail is reinventing letter and mail delivery by destroying time and space;
» Internet chatlines and the Web may well be reinventing all of the above; and
» in less than two years, CDs destroyed the "record album and disk" market that had thrived and existed for at least 80 years!

The rules of global innovation have changed; there's been an innovation in innovation

Now back to global innovation. Global innovation is more than simply creating a new product or service, which of course is no easy task in itself. Global innovation involves meeting more requirements or taking more issues or interests into consideration than offering customers something new. Meeting the ISO 9000 quality management standards is now a requirement for doing business globally. ISO 14000, the environmental management set of standards, is not far behind ISO 9000 in becoming a basic entry test for doing business globally. With the addition of those two sets of expectations, global innovation has changed dramatically. The nine principles of the Global Compact mentioned in Chapter 1 are also changing the meaning of global innovation.

The nine principles of the Global Compact, again, are:

» *Principle 1*: supporting and respecting the protection of international human rights within their sphere of influence;
» *Principle 2*: ensuring their own corporations are not complicit in human rights abuses;
» *Principle 3*: freedom of association and the effective recognition of the right to collective bargaining;
» *Principle 4*: the elimination of all forms of forced and compulsory labor;
» *Principle 5*: the effective abolition of child labor;
» *Principle 6*: the elimination of discrimination in respect of employment and occupation;
» *Principle 7*: supporting a precautionary approach to environmental challenges;
» *Principle 8*: undertaking initiatives to promote greater environmental responsibility; and
» *Principle 9*: encouraging the development and diffusion of environmentally friendly technologies.

SCOUTING THE FUTURE AND SCOUTING YOUR WAY TO SUCCESS

The greatest challenges of global innovation, however, have not changed. "Getting out of the box" or out of your comfort zone to see the future or reinvent yourself, your products, or your services is still one of the greatest innovation challenges.

We believe that a set of methods or practices that fit under the term "scouting" offers the most practical way to approach innovation.

SCOUTING THE PAST TO LEARN ABOUT HOW TO MANAGE THE FUTURE

Royal Dutch Shell's former strategic planning chief Arie P. de Geus, in a paper prepared for a learning organization conference of the Rotterdam School of Management and the European Learning Network, notes that Shell learned about anticipating the future by "scouting" the past. He notes:

"the Shell planning group conducted a study of 'the corporate survivors' – companies which should inspire Shell, which were older than Shell, and relatively as important in their industry as Shell is in the oil industry.

"One of several interesting findings of this study is that these companies vary in age from 100 to 700 years. Compared to the average life expectancy of 40 to 50 years, it appears that there is considerable scope for improvement.

"Each of these companies had gone through some fundamental environmental change and had survived with their corporate identity intact. Some of the older companies like the Swedish Stora have had their ups and downs as a result of changes in the world over its 700 years of existence, but, remarkably, most of the time they had picked up the signals of major change and had acted on them before it had become an unmanageable crisis.

"Managing internal change by foresight, rather than by crisis is only possible if the change in the environment is seen on time."

Professor Hidaki Yoshihara doesn't use the term "scouting" but he describes in a different way what we mean by scouting. He says: "Shutting up oneself in one's own small world is not a good thing. It is necessary to look outside, to look at the great world that surrounds us. Please watch what is going on in the United States, Japan, and other foreign countries. Look at industries apart from your own. Try to understand historical, long-term trends, and ride on them." He recommends that managers write the answers to their test, in effect, by looking at how other companies answered the same types of questions. He says, "The world, our society, is not evenly developed. There are advanced places and backward places. Writing his or her company's test sheet while looking at the answers given by more advanced companies is part of a manager's job."

Scouting is a collection of methods used to facilitate innovation. Scouting includes individual and organizational activities related to scanning the perceived and simulated horizons for ideas, new and old, which may have implications for the organization. Scouting can be viewed in a number of ways. Scouting may be considered as:

» a new application of an old concept;
» a system with associated subsystems and functions;
» a process with associated subprocesses;
» a set of forms;
» a set of focuses; and
» a different way to organize to serve customers or obtain information.

Functions of scouting

1 *Environmental scanning*: The primary function of scouting is "scanning" the organization's internal and external environments for information and knowledge. This is used to help the CEO and the executive team fine-tune the firm's alignment for future change.

   Macro-scouting involves scanning a very broad set of areas external to the organization. These areas include technologies, lifestyles, and cultural trends. Macro-scouting involves a somewhat different type of mind focus, and consideration of seemingly unrelated developments. One must be able to imagine how these factors could impact upon the firm. The search conference method, as we will see later on, is an excellent way to organize macro-scouting.

Micro-scouting focuses on specific present and emergent trends, issues, and disciplines of knowledge to determine their future implications relative to the vision of the firm. Individuals performing micro-focus scouting need knowledge in their specific discipline or skill set.

2 *Developing "possible futures" scenarios*: Scouting may be used to scan a broad range of knowledge, global practices, and emergent processes to conceptualize alternative futures. These alternatives could then be examined to ascertain their implications for the organization's future direction and priorities.

3 *Supporting organizational learning*: For organizations to discover new opportunities to create their futures, they must develop innovative learning systems. Such activities include the creation of new conceptual maps, which integrate past knowledge.

Shell's former strategic planning chief, Arie de Geus says, "it is possible to make micro worlds of a company, or of its market, its competition, etc. with which management can experiment without having to fear the consequences. Like the pilot in the flight simulator, they can take the company through extreme situations to find out in the process the existence of options which they would normally have avoided in the classical boardroom situation."

4 *Scouting is an open-ended and continuing process*: It does not seek a final solution. Scouting incorporates many aspects of traditional reconnoitering. Webster's dictionary states that to reconnoiter is to survey, examine, or "to carry out a reconnaissance." Thus, scouting supports renewal through reconnoitering new information.

5 *Scouting involves the process of discovering what exists now and what is emerging*: This is what the Japanese call *sunao*, "the untrapped mind." *Sunao* involves seeing the world as it is in a moment-to-moment sense. To perceive the world as it is, one must have the ability to scan the world from an inner state of non-attachment. Scouting from a *sunao* perspective involves "being more and doing less."

Warren Bennis emphasizes the importance of "operating on instinct" and listening to the "inner voice." For example, being and reflection has become a way of life at Patagonia, Inc., a mail order firm of sports wear. Founder Yvon Chouinard exemplifies the importance of self-expression and following one's inner voice by spending six months away from the firm every year. Chouinard spends time reflecting, relaxing, testing the firm's products, and dreaming about new products. Chouinard does not feel the need to prove himself by adopting the conventional practices of more traditional executives.

"WHAT'S NEW?" HAS MORE THAN ONE MEANING!

A challenge that is separate and at the same time part and parcel of getting out of the box, is understanding what customers mean when they ask, "what's new?"

When employees, customers, suppliers, communities, etc. ask what's new, we have found that they have nine factors in mind, each of which may be weighted differently for different products and services or in their interactions with your company.

We have also found that most if not all of these factors are based on or colored by two of the most basic human drives.

As psycho-biological beings, all humans are "wired" or "encoded" to:

1 survive, reproduce, and do nothing to threaten the survival of our species; and
2 seek out new experiences, and create/learn new ways to do things, both for pure enjoyment and to become more adaptable – enhancing the ability of our species to survive.

In simpler language, we hope, this translates into:

» the need/urge to create or experience new phenomena and new ways of meeting old and "new" needs; and
» the need/urge to be able to predict outcomes and the environment.

As you will see below, at times these two drives or needs are so closely intertwined that it is difficult to determine which aspect is more important

You may have wondered why we noted the innovation in terror in the introduction. It comes into play here. The threat or change in the world system may well cause people to look for "new" ways to assure predictability, control, and security in different aspects of their life and work.

THE DRIVERS OF INNOVATION

1 *I want to have greater input into the services and products I buy. I want more input into how my community is run, I want greater input in my worklife.* This is the result of a deep desire to express and apply democratic ideals in every aspect of our lives and society. Can you think of any institution or structure in our society where our beliefs in democracy are not trying to express themselves? All aspects of society are touched by it. It's not democracy with a big D and it doesn't mean that people want to vote on all decisions.

2 *I want it my way!* Newness is not the only driver of the market or management approaches. Many consumers and employees are also saying "I want it my way!"

From fast food to cars, bicycles, clothing, and jobs, people want the convenience, cost, and quality of mass production and in just the way they want it – customized just for them! The challenge has become: either figure out how to mass produce high-quality, low-cost customized products and services or become a niche or speciality firm.

3 *Low cost and high quality are no longer separate choices.* Consumers know that they can expect and demand both low cost and high quality. This expectation is working its way through the global society and its organizations in a steady manner. In short, people will no longer accept shoddy goods or service (even in government) for long from anyone.

4 *"What's new?"* The irrepressible urge for all things new and shiny. Two people who have not seen each other for a week or so approach each other on the street. One says, "What's new?" The other says, "Nothing much." The first person may think or even say, "Oh, that's too bad." What's new is both a blessing and a curse. It's good because it drives people to tinker and improve things; it's bad when it pressures people to think that something they do or have is deficient because it's not brand new.

5 *Is it user-friendly?* The customer still wants products and services that are user-friendly. Why? Because very few of us really want to

solve puzzling manuals, dials, or automated telephone gateways to get to use the product or service we want or need. The one solid rule, that everyone should never, never, never forget is this: if you make the product or service easier to use or access, customers will select your product or service over another.

6 *Is it Earth-friendly?* This is no longer a nice place to be. As we come to better understand systems and ecology, we are quickly learning that we can't stand outside of nature or its systems. As we have noted above, this is a key aspect of the Global Compact and the very reason ISO 14000 is growing in importance.

7 *Is it people-friendly?* This is similar to the Earth-friendly requirement. Is your product or service, or company harmful, neutral, or beneficial to people at work and not disrupting their community or economy?

8 *Is it beautiful or elegant?* No surprise here, is there? The problem is that this common desire on the part of customers aligns with the What's new? factor. People's ideas of what is beautiful or elegant keep changing. We will not do much with this one, except to say that elegance is related to simplicity, which is also related to user-friendliness.

9 *Can we trust you?* The trust and loyalty that once seemed to be almost automatically accorded to organizations and institutions now must be earned over and over again. This is not a pleasant state of affairs. But it is a natural reaction by nearly everyone when they have seen their particular ideal community or society fall or falter under the onslaught of outside forces or due to internal decay. It is a dynamic that causes very real emotional pain for those who are consistently ethical and compassionate in dealing with others. Nevertheless, it is real and cannot be ignored. At times, it seems there is a zero tolerance for any error, deviation, or lapse.

The Road from Innovation to Global Innovation and on to Global Innovation Plus

» The technical/scientific drivers of global innovation.
» The social and political drivers of global innovation.
» The connections between Gandhi, Phil Knight, and the Global Compact.
» Global innovation time-line.

When Alexander Graham Bell invented the telephone, the news of it took weeks, months, and years to reach every community in the world. In the US, market penetration of the telephone did not close in on 90%-plus until the early 1950s.

Today, hypothetically, when a new, faster, and safer way to repair a common knee injury is developed, proven, and reported by a surgical team in Sweden, it takes less than 24 hours for the news to reach every news service in the world. It may then take less than an hour or two for someone covered by national healthcare insurance in the US (or in Canada, Singapore, Japan, the UK, or many other countries) to call his surgeon and ask whether he can have that procedure rather than the "traditional" one recommended by the surgeon last week. This surgeon's response further illustrates the sea changes in global innovation from Alexander Graham Bell till today.

She says to her patient, "I read about that too. I have been watching for and expecting a new method such as this because of all the advances in micro-laser technology in the last year or two. I assumed that you or one of my other patients would be calling, so I checked it out on the Internet. I found out that:

1 hands-on training in the new procedure begins there in two weeks;
2 hands-on training here in South Beach by someone trained there will probably begin in a month or two;
3 virtual, computer-based training will probably be available in three or four months.

"I can refer you to that surgical practice. They already have a six to ten week waiting period. I checked with the insurance board and found out that the cost of the procedure will be covered. You would have to cover the travel costs, of course.

"The choice of when you want the new procedure done is up to you. I have already booked myself for hands-on training there next month, since I have a number of patients that will benefit and will be calling me about it as you have. So, the choice is yours. What would you like to do?"

There are two sets of drivers illustrated by our historical and hypothetical examples: technical/scientific drivers and social/political drivers.

THE TECHNICAL/SCIENTIFIC DRIVERS OF GLOBAL INNOVATION

No, we are not going to recount the evolution of the entire range of technical and scientific innovation. The advances/innovations in communications (as well as in information processing and analysis), transportation, and mass production are those that have driven the changes in global innovation. They have dramatically reduced both the cost and the time it takes for what had been a "local" innovation to become a global innovation. While there are literally thousands of examples of how innovations in these areas have reduced costs and almost erased time as a limiter to innovation, one which one of the authors experienced just recently will well illustrate how much the innovation landscape has shifted in a very short time.

A prospective subscriber to a management journal, from a manufacturing institute in Bangalore, India, e-mailed requesting a sample copy. The journal is edited and "printed" in Cincinnati, Ohio in the US. When a similar request was made six or seven years ago, it took nearly two weeks for the mail to arrive in Cincinnati. Then it took nearly the same amount of time for the sample paper journal to arrive in Bangalore – the cost of mailing the single copy of the journal and its production costs (less overhead) was approximately $15.00 (and the cost of the subscription was substantially higher than in North America).

The editor's reply to this recent inquiry was to e-mail back and ask if it would be all right to send the sample issue as a PDF (portable document format that can be read via a free electronic reader on the requester's PC) attachment to another e-mail. In the same e-mail, the editor informed the potential customer that an electronic subscription cost less than the paper version and could be read online, or downloaded for reading on his PC or printing. He also noted that the subscription could be made online and that he could probably be reading their first issue or scanning past issues – also online – the following day. The cost (less overhead) to send out the sample and to "deliver" the subscription? Even though a "cost" could be assigned to sending the sample and providing the subscription, for all practical purposes those costs are now figured at zero in comparison to the costs in the past.

The production and delivery costs of many other types of products are, of course, substantial. The costs and time to either deliver information about the product or service or acquire that information as a private customer or as a B2B (business-to-business) customer have, in comparison to what was required six or seven years ago, declined so much that global innovation is almost instantaneous, or seemingly so.

The demonstration effect of an innovation in your field drives the next one – both faster than before and from around the world. Why? Because some existing customers, potential customers, suppliers, and competitors either read about the innovation on the Internet, or because of the Internet and cable and satellite communications they hear about it on the radio or television and are soon asking for it or expecting it to be available for purchase from you.

The advances during the 1970s, 1980s, and 1990s in quality and mass production almost totally changed customers' expectations about when they might be able to both afford and take delivery of the latest consumer electronics innovation. The advances were quite dramatic and taught by demonstration effect that the customer should be able to expect the same speed and drop in costs as soon as the product got out of the early adopter stage.

The most dramatic advances have come in just the last six years – since 1995. Why 1995? That was the year that:

» the World Wide Web (WWW) surpassed ftp-data in March as the service with greatest traffic on NSFNet based on packet count, and in April based on byte count; and

» online dial-up systems (Compuserve, America Online, Prodigy) began to provide Internet access.[1]

After 1995, the social/political drivers of global innovation, in effect, shift global innovation into some sort of "hyperdrive," to borrow a term from science fiction.

We believe, and think you will soon agree, if you do not already, that social/political innovations or changes have been the real drivers of global innovation and are now even more so. In the popular and scientific media, most of the attention is focused on the technical and scientific aspects of innovation. There are two reasons for that. One is that it is difficult to "show" the process and collection of people it takes to create an innovation. The second reason is that the people actually involved with creating or researching technical innovations are more interested and often find it easier to talk about the technical/scientific aspects of their innovation. But ask them how they achieved it or why and, again, as often as not, you will get an answer that reveals the social/political drivers. The CEO of Medtronics has said that what drives her to innovate is her desire to spare other daughters and sons from experiencing the grief of a father dying from the lack of appropriate medical technology.

THE SOCIAL AND POLITICAL DRIVERS OF GLOBAL INNOVATION

The three most historically important drivers of innovation over the past 100 years, even more dramatic over the past 10 years or so, are:

1 the expansion of political democracy and the attendant expectation that all social institutions should be in some sense democratic or participative;
2 the rise of many different types of mass social movements; and
3 innovations in leading, managing, and organizing people to produce goods and services.

THE CONNECTIONS BETWEEN GANDHI, PHIL KNIGHT, AND THE GLOBAL COMPACT

A brief race through the connections between Gandhi's use of civil disobedience and non-violent resistance and Nike CEO Phil Knight's support for the Global Compact will serve to illustrate how social and political changes both drive global innovation and have shifted it so much that we are referring to it as "global innovation plus."

For those born since 1970 or so, we are talking about Mohandas "Mahatma" Gandhi, one of the chief strategists and leaders of India's drive for independence from Great Britain. India became independent in 1948-9 after an active struggle that spanned nearly 50 years. Gandhi's most effective means of resisting the British and gathering support for his country's independence within his nation, from English voters, and from supporters around the world – who would exert pressure on

Great Britain to set India free – was the use of both individual and mass civil disobedience and non-violent resistance. Gandhi did not "invent" either method but his use, explanation, and refinement of methods "demonstrated" by labor unions was his "social innovation."

The United States is not the inventor of political democracy, but since 1789, with the establishment of its constitution, it had been a leading innovator in expanding democracy – for "white" males. Civil rights for African-Americans became a mass movement in the early 1960s when the Reverend Martin Luther King, Jr took his understanding of Gandhi's methods and began applying them to advancing civil rights for African-Americans in the US.

Among the many supporters of the American Civil Rights Movement were people with growing interests in women's rights, in environmental issues, in opposing the growing US involvement in the war in Viet Nam, in making products safer and more reliable, in civil rights for Mexican-Americans, in civil rights for American Indians, etc.

The activities of all these movements were reported by the mass media in the US and since the US had become the most powerful economic and political player on the world scene following World War II, these mass movements were reported on worldwide. When the US Environmental Agency was founded in 1970, the demonstration effect of the successful use of Gandhi's/King's methods on environmental issues alone gave life to duplicate efforts in societies around the world. The combination of support for civil and human rights by labor unions and anti-war activists helped to fuel and nurture international support for human rights. So, we can see that the distance between Gandhi's philosophy and social-political innovations and Nike being supportive of the Global Compact was bridged by the demonstration effect of Martin Luther King's use and refinement of Gandhi's methods on people who then used that social-political innovation to advance their interest in a number of different causes that come together and are represented in the nine principles of the Global Compact.

The people involved in those mass movements never stopped being consumers either. They wanted to purchase goods and services from those who supported their interests, as well as goods and services that expressed their interests or were the result of their efforts. The result was that many companies thought of as being innovative were formed to serve the interests of those involved in the social-political movement by adherence to the issue, or were companies that recognized the market opportunity for new products and services that these people represented.

Add to this one more significant fact, that many of these people did not leave their interests at home when they went to work. They have, and continue to look for, ways to either express those concerns in their work or to make their companies fit their changed view of the world. In our surgical example, not a few of the readers have already made the connection. If there had been no renewed women's or feminist movement during the 1970s, the chances that our patient in need of knee surgery would be consulting by choice with a female surgeon would be vastly reduced in many cultures.

The learning here is that you need to scout beyond your competitors, your own field. What is happening in the larger society has changed your landscape in the past and will do so in the future as well. At the same time, scouting is a rich source for ideas, for global innovations of your own in what you produce, how you produce it, to whom are you going to sell it, and how you will organize to deliver it.

The time-line below combines the technical/scientific with the social/political. As a result, it is much abbreviated, since otherwise it would soon overwhelm this book and could indeed be a book or study of its own.

Some have written that the automobile changed the face of the world. Actually, the automobile did nothing. What changed the face of the world is where people wanted to drive, how fast and smoothly, how safely, who and what they wanted to carry along with them, and their desire to express their personality or self-esteem with their vehicle. They turned those interests into demands of auto-makers.

GLOBAL INNOVATION TIME-LINE

Note: Each society has its own history of establishing measures and means to assure quality of goods and services. The very early examples are just that: a few early examples of how and when measures were established. The advance in quality and quality management is often noted simply by the publication date of a book significant to the movement.

» **1876**: Alexander Graham Bell and Thomas Watson exhibit an electric telephone.
» **1889**: Automobile: Karl Benz.
» **1895**: Wireless telegraph: Guglielmo Marconi.
» **1903**: Orville Wright and Wilbur Wright fly the first motor-driven airplane.
» **1908**: Henry Ford develops the assembly line method of automobile manufacturing.
» **1919**: The International Labour Organization (ILO) is established to advocate human rights represented in labor law, encompassing concerns such as employment discrimination, forced labor, and worker safety.
» **1920**: Difference engine: Charles Babbage; 19th Amendment, granting women's votes, adopted; analog telephone facsimile - digital facsimile between 1920 and 1923.
» **1923**: The Equal Rights Amendment was introduced into Congress.
» **1927**: British Broadcasting Corporation established.
» **1939–45**: Second World War.
» **1945**: The United Nations (UN) is established. Its Charter states that one of its main purposes is the promotion and encouragement of "respect for human rights and for fundamental freedoms for all without distinction as to race, sex, language or religion."
» **1946**: Commission on Human Rights established by the UN Economic and Social Council (ECOSOC).
» **1947**: First supersonic flight.
» **1948**: UN General Assembly adopts the Universal Declaration of Human Rights.
» **1949**: Convention on the Right to Organize and Collective Bargaining (ILO) is adopted.
» **1957**: The United States Congress approves a civil rights bill, to protect voting rights for African-Americans. It is the first civil rights bill since the Reconstruction period, which immediately

followed the Civil War. Toyota Motor Sales, USA, Inc. (TMS) begins operations in US.

» **1958**: Chester Carlson presents the first photocopier suitable for office use.
» **1961**: Honda introduces motorbikes in US.
» **1962**: *Silent Spring* by Rachel Carson published.
» **1964**: The Omnibus Civil Rights Bill banning discrimination in voting, jobs, public accommodation, and other activities, is adopted; Martin Luther King, Jr wins the Nobel Peace Prize; anti-war movement in US begins ''teach-ins.''
» **1965**: A new Voting Rights Act authorizes the US government to appoint examiners to register voters where local officials have made African-American registration difficult.
» **1969**: ARPANET commissioned by DoD for research into networking.
» **1970**: Computer-scanned binary signal code first used (aka ''barcodes''); the Equal Rights Amendment is reintroduced to US Congress; Earth Day; Clean Air Act passed in US; Environmental Protection Agency established.
» **1973**: Endangered Species Act passed in US; treaty ending war in Viet Nam is signed; OPEC raises cost of oil from $3 to $12 – begins economic crisis.
» **1974**: Bill Gates and Paul Allen write a version of BASIC for the Altair computer and start a company called Microsoft Corporation.
» **1975**: Development of Beta VCR system by Sony, Japan; and the VHS system by Matsushita, Japan.
» **1977**: Apple II, the first home computer, by Steve Jobs and Steve Wozniak; a Human Rights Bureau is created within the United States Department of State. Its first reports on human rights are issued that year; Amnesty International wins the Nobel Peace Prize.
» **1979**: VisiCalc, first spreadsheet program, Apple II; Three Mile Island nuclear power plant almost had a meltdown, giving the nuclear power industry a permanent black eye in US.
» **1980**: Nissan Motor Manufacturing Corp., USA established.

» **1981**: IBM introduced the IBM PC.

» **1982**: Compaq introduced the first IBM-compatible machine.

» **1984**: Domain Name System (DNS) introduced; number of hosts breaks 1000; New United Motor Manufacturing, Inc. (NUMMI), a Toyota joint venture with General Motors, begins operations in US.

» **1985**: Whole Earth 'Lectronic Link (WELL) started.

» **1986**: The Number Four reactor at Chernobyl suffers a disastrous explosion and fire.

» **1987**: ISO 9000 is published.

» **1989**: Number of hosts breaks 100,000; in Tiananmen Square, Chinese authorities massacre student demonstrators struggling for democracy; Dalai Lama wins the Nobel Peace Prize; Exxon Valdez disaster; Berlin Wall falls; Soichiro Honda, founder of Honda, is inducted into the Automotive Hall of Fame (USA).

» **1990**: The Americans With Disabilities Act is signed into law.

» **1991**: Wide Area Information Servers (WAIS), invented by Brewster Kahle, released by Thinking Machines Corporation; Gopher released by Paul Lindner and Mark P. McCahill from the University of Minnesota; World Wide Web (WWW) released by CERN, Tim Berners-Lee developer; 300,000 unionists march in Washington, DC to demand workplace fairness and healthcare reform; Soviet Union is dissolved.

» **1994–2005**: UN Decade for Human Rights Education is declared on December 23 (UN); *The Fifth Discipline* by Peter Senge published.

» **1995**: WWW surpasses ftp-data in March as the service with greatest traffic on NSFNet based on packet count, and in April based on byte count; traditional online dial-up systems (Compuserve, America Online, Prodigy) begin to provide Internet access; Beijing Declaration at the World Conference on Women declares "Women's rights are human rights."

» **2000**: ISO 9000 is revised; Global Compact is established by UN Secretary-General.

WWW growth

» 06/95: 23,500 sites.
» 06/98: 2,410,067 sites.
» 06/99: 6,177,453 sites.
» 06/00: 17,119,262 sites.
» 06/01: 29,302,656 sites.

NOTE

1 Source: Robert "Hobbes" Zakon, e-mail: Robert@Zakon.org, Website: www.Zakon.org.

Global Innovation and the E-Dimension: What's the Connection?

» The indivisibility effect.
» Corporate investment in information technology.
» Destroying time and space.
» Global innovations in infrastructure, the backbone of organizations.
» Best practice: EDI at Standard Life.
» The Internet's challenge.

The e-dimension's connection or impact on global innovation is so basic, such an indivisible aspect of global innovation, that it is a bit difficult to think of it as a separate aspect of global innovation. The hard and soft technologies that make up the e-dimension of business and government are at one and the same time the facilitators of global innovation and global innovations themselves.

The impact of the 1960s transistor as a global innovation may seem to be ancient history to some, but its effect on telephones, radio, television, and business devices has been so great it is nearly immeasurable. The same might be said of integrated chips. The miniaturization and portability they gave birth to were, and still are, strategic principles of global innovation. Making the device smaller and cheaper meant that devices beyond our imagination at times now make use of computers and telecommunications. The technology can enable continuous health monitoring of a patient as they go to work and travel about the city, helps keep the airport for Hong Kong on the level, and enables the weekend carpenter via his electronic hand-held to be absolutely sure that the deck being added on to his home is also level.

The chief means of communicating news and information about global innovation, television, telephones, and radio (telecommunication – the first "converged technology"), are the result of a number of global innovations and continue to be the subject of innovation. The addition of computers and a network of communication satellites to those technologies has meant that the news and detailed information about innovations now reach potential innovators and consumers of innovations around the world 24 hours a day and seven days a week.

The announcement in Tel Aviv, San Jose, Stockholm, Berlin, Kobe, or Helsinki of a hand-held, pen-size device that enables someone to scan text for storage and later downloading to a computer, not only sparks a call or e-mail by a consumer in Durban, South Africa to a local retail electronics store asking when she can purchase one, it may cause the manager of a social program for the blind, or nearly blind, to call or e-mail an engineer friend in a technology company and suggest that if they could connect that device with existing inexpensive voice-capable software and a hand-held computer with a speaker, his clients could "read" nearly anything and anywhere. "That would," the manager might say, "add so greatly to our people's work and social world that it's hard to imagine – can you do it – soon?"

CORPORATE INVESTMENT IN INFORMATION TECHNOLOGY

Corporate investment in information technology demonstrates that the connection between the e-dimension and global innovation has become as significant, or more so, than any other type of investment to support and drive production. Professor Danny Tyson Quah of the London School of Economics noted in a paper prepared for delivery at a conference in 1997:

> "Over the last three decades (between 1970 and 1996) business investment in IT hardware as a fraction of total investment increased six-fold from 7% to 40%. Combined with software expenditures, this fraction has grown to exceed (the share of) investment in all physical machinery."

In plain English, companies have "voted" with their investments and decided that e-devices and software are essential to the daily running of businesses and in enabling them to globally innovate.

The race of technology forward and the amount of money invested in it makes it easy for all of us to underestimate the importance of the h-dimension of global innovation – that is, the human dimension.

DESTROYING TIME AND SPACE

Global innovations in communications and information processing have in one sense destroyed time and distance as significant limits to our abilities. We have the capability to monitor and "manage" business services and production in Chicago, Calgary, Calcutta, Capetown, Coventry, and Cairo from an office in Boston or Bogota in real time. However, we have to ask ourselves about gaps between capability and actual ability. Many, if not most, companies are still "organized" around a management model developed when the world was shocked by the sinking of the "unsinkable" *Titanic* and marveled that the telegraph enabled us to learn about the disaster, almost as if we were there.

A military commander at NATO headquarters in Belgium has the capability to "electronically" and in real time watch forces in the field in the Balkans, Africa, or Asia. A stock trader has the ability to monitor and conduct stock trading activities around the world, 24 hours a day. Both the commander and the trader have the capability to make a decision and almost "instantly" see it enacted and judge whether the decision was correct or not. In addition, since CNN, AP, or Reuters reporters are watching and reporting on the activities of the stock trades, the NATO commander, and opposition soldiers in the field, the public, investors, and government agencies are able to "instantly" make judgments on the activities of the stock trader and the commander.

In short, technological and global innovation have given us great capabilities. The challenge is whether we have the abilities in human terms to use those innovations responsibly and effectively.

As a consumer or client of a large organization, you know at some level that an instant decision can be made on your request or initiating action. This creates a demand and an opportunity for "instant" reaction by the company or agency. The challenge and balancing point is whether our human organization is organized to meet those changing demands and conditions effectively. Does the clerk or front-line person have the training, resources, and authority to respond appropriately, or does he or she have to use a human system designed to meet the conditions and requirements of the 1940s or 50s instead of 2000?

Global technical innovations in one part of an organization's system create demands that the rest of the system, and especially the human system, is both capable and able to respond to in kind. Federal Express and American Express gained significant competitive advantage in their respective fields because their frontline people had the capability, ability, and authority to act on consumer needs and demands in real time rather than wait for six levels and days for decisions. They are excellent examples of global social or human systems innovations that used global technological innovations to adapt to and satisfy customer needs or requirements.

GLOBAL INNOVATIONS IN INFRASTRUCTURE, THE BACKBONE OF ORGANIZATIONS

Electronic data interchange (EDI) gives companies and governments the ability to make transactions with them easier and faster for customers and clients and at the same time dramatically cut the time and cost to act on the information or requests communicated.

EDI DEFINED

EDI enables companies which have processed data electronically internally to exchange this data with other companies or organizations. EDI trading partners seldom communicate directly, but use a third-party Value-Added Network (VAN). VANs provide a communications network to connect trading partners, regardless of individual hardware platforms or communications protocols. Each partner connects to the VAN, and the VAN manages the connections to all the trading partners.

VANs also serve as a document clearing-house, either providing a mailbox service to store received interchanges until a user is ready to download them, or proactively delivering interchanges to a user. For example, a user can request immediate delivery of all purchase orders, or request delivery of all interchanges from XYZ Company at 3.00 p.m.

The best practice case below demonstrates how an infrastructure innovation can support an innovation in speed of service for clients.

BEST PRACTICE: EDI AT STANDARD LIFE

Standard Life, with more than 12,000 employees worldwide and 7300 staff based in Edinburgh, is one of the leading mutual financial service companies in the world and Scotland's largest private employer. In 1997/8 it sold 529,000 policies in the UK, with a total new premium income of over £1bn. Although more than 170 years old, it is a modern multinational company.

Standard Life wanted to move away from the paper reporting system and the time spent by staff in processing three types of tax documents, by implementing an EDI system. There was also a need to reduce the number of errors.

» *Before EDI*: Standard Life ran a payments system with over 100,000 annuity records. Prior to implementing EDI, the manual workload was carried out using internal resources only, with an error rate of 28% just on one type of incoming form. In another area 18,000 forms sent to the Inland Revenue annually were prepared and dispatched manually. Data capture of 90,000 coding notifications a year involved a large amount of checking and verification to ensure data validity. As a result, it could take up to a week to get a document entered onto the relevant computer system. Standard Life reported that the costs involved to process two forms alone were estimated to be tens of thousands of pounds per annum, involving over 1000 man-hours.
» *After EDI*: Inbound messages of one type are currently received from the Inland Revenue on a daily basis. Outbound data from two other forms is now batch-processed overnight and transmitted to the Inland Revenue on a daily basis.
» *Overall benefits*: The actual benefits achieved were:
  » a paperless environment with fast (automated), efficient application of data and electronic data storage;
  » improved accuracy of data reporting allied with error reduction;
  » financial and operational integrity;
  » improvement in the audit trails with "guaranteed" data receipt;
  » an increase in data integrity, including Inland Revenue files; and
  » a reduction in postal and stationery costs.[1]

THE INTERNET'S CHALLENGE

The Internet is a global innovation that has enabled companies to start up and exist, in a sense, virtually, since they are based on storefronts that are electronic only, as compared with "bricks-and-mortar" stores. The advantage was thought to be unlimited. However, the inability of Internet companies to deliver goods and services on time and correctly led to them going out of business almost as quickly as they entered.

Companies that have learned from the errors of those early Internet companies will, however, continue to recreate business after business. Barnes & Noble has responded well to the challenge of cyber-based Amazon.com by offering an online experience as good as Amazon's and by advertising their services and capabilities in traditional as well as Web media. Amazon.com continues to innovate in ways that mimic a customer's ability to scan a book as they would in a bricks-and-mortar store and talk with other people about the book, CD, or DVD via chat rooms, customer reviews, and customers' "best of" lists.

Then there is the struggle in the music and film industry to determine how best to adapt to the digitalization of its product and the seemingly almost infinite number of ways to define or categorize its product in terms of its devotees. For example, the customer who is only interested in techno-tribal music can find groups and samples of music all over the world via the Internet. Bricks-and-mortar as well as cyber-stores are adapting to enable that customer to order sets of pre-packaged selections that may be mailed as a cyber or solid product. The sticking point at present is that the customer has difficulty in selecting his or her own package and having a choice of delivery and media.

The most promising aspects of doing business on the Internet are:

» the ability of companies to customize their product or service;
» the ability of speciality or niche companies to enable customers around the globe to "find" them; and
» the ability to invite customers and suppliers into the design of new products and services via Internet-enabled conversations and simulations.

The challenge to deliver on those abilities is not limited to technical global innovations. Innovations in how companies are organized to deliver service and product are equally promising, as are innovations in how their employees are empowered and resourced to deliver.

NOTE

1 Source: http://www.inlandrevenue.gov.uk/ebu/case1.htm.

What are the Implications of Globalization and the Issues it Raises?

- » A glass half empty and half full: global education.
- » Global institutions.
- » Best practice case: the Integrated Rural Development (IRD) program in Ireland.

Not long ago, the BBC ran a feature on its worldwide radio broad-cast about Britons planning to purchase a package offering the customer's/patient's desired cosmetic surgery with an extended safari. The "surgery safari" offered was reported to be attractive to those who wanted to cover their cosmetic visit with a perfectly "socially accepted" vacation. The bonus was that the combined cost, because of currency exchange and labor cost differences, was less than the surgery alone at a private practice in Great Britain.

To those who may well think that "global" innovations in marketing cosmetic surgery is trivial, the message is this – the marketers are counting on that attitude, since it will help them sell their services to those sensitive to peer pressures in the UK and other countries where people can afford the "non-essential" medical service offered.

What are the implications of globalization on global innovation? We know that this may seem to be begging the question, since it seems that, by definition, global is global. The difference here is that, in the not too distant past when you read about global innovations in particular fields, they tended to come out of one, two, or three countries, or possibly economic regions. If not today, soon there will be no such human endeavor one can think of, from fresh and prepared foods available at a local grocer's or restaurant to medical procedures developed in one corner of the globe and "transported" via both for-profit and not-for-profit training in months – not years, as in the past.

ISO 9000 has always been an international standard designed, in part, to promote global trade. So there's a bit of irony in the fact that ISO has been playing catch-up with various industries like auto and medical devices and has devised global standards for its industry-specific variants of ISO 9000 – itself a global standard.

Let's take a step back for a macro-global view of why global innovation today and in the near future is more global than ever before – meaning that the innovation may arise in more places and go global faster than ever before.

A GLASS HALF EMPTY AND HALF FULL: GLOBAL EDUCATION

The fact that so many millions worldwide are still not literate and able to fully participate in or take advantage of the employment opportunities now available is real and is driving educators around the globe to seek more funding and different ways of funding basic education. It is also driving educators and entrepreneurs around the globe to develop innovations in how education is delivered and how children and adults are taught. In this case, it is a lack or a negative that drives innovation. So, we see institutions all over the globe experimenting and developing "distance learning." The breakthroughs or innovations may come from any part of the globe. Why? Because the glass is also half full, not just half empty.

According to UNESCO's Institute for Statistics, in 1970 there were 28,084 thousand students enrolled worldwide in post-secondary education. In 1997, there were 88,156 thousand. The worldwide number represents an impressive gain. The gain is even more impressive when one considers the increases in areas that are considered less developed (Table 5.1).

Table 5.1 Students enrolled in post-secondary education: developing countries (source: http://www.uis.unesco.org/statsen/statistics/yearbook/tables/).

Year	Students enrolled in post-secondary education
1970	6,956 thousand
1997	43,357 thousand

The point is that there are more people worldwide, including developing countries with post-secondary education, than ever before in history and in more parts of the world than ever before. These are not the only source for inventors and innovators, to be sure. They are, however, the source for leading, organizing, and managing companies and agencies.

Or think about it this way. In this year alone, some 43,000 thousand more people in the developing world (students who may have just graduated in 2001 from university or technical school in developing countries), 88,000 thousand when you count the whole world, are now potentially thinking about how to create a global innovation in their area of interest – or being paid to do so – than last year. That is an enormous change in just three decades.

There are engineering schools, medical schools, business schools, and a host of technical schools, regularly turning out fresh minds in more countries than ever before in history. That has to have an impact on your ability to innovate – more human capacity – and means that innovation may come from almost any direction and faster than you might have expected.

Any direction and faster? Yes, coming from any direction and faster because of the growth in global institutions and networks that co-operate in fostering innovation, nurturing environments for innovation, and spreading/sharing/offering information and knowledge.

GLOBAL INSTITUTIONS

Just consider the impact of three global institutions and their impact on global innovation in their area of expertise or interest: the International Labour Organization, The World Health Organization, and the International Organization for Standardization (ISO). Discounting innovations that these institutions may have fostered in supporting research and development themselves, the sharing of best practices and basic information on developments around the world via publications and conferences has meant the information and knowledge was diffused farther and faster than ever before in human history (before the Internet became a factor, which may well have raised those rates by a factor of 5, 10, or more – it's difficult to guess or estimate).

Just consider a few social or political innovations, not strictly commercial or technological innovations. A labor organizer in Cambodia needs help in developing a new strategy to communicate with labor contractors or prospective members. He or she places a call, sends a fax, or e-mails a network he learned about at an ILO conference or read about in one of their publications. The next morning, six different solutions may have arrived from different parts of the globe. Or the opposite: she or he develops a new way to communicate effectively with the same parties and posts the method to a network via one or all of the same means – within 24 hours it is available worldwide.

The informal "race" to find the cause of what became known as AIDS was a two-continent race in the 1980s between researchers in the US and France. The first useful drug, AZT, was developed by Glaxo

Wellcome (then Burroughs Wellcome), a British firm, and manufactured at its Greenville, North Carolina, USA plant.

When there is an outbreak of Ebola today, an emergency response team is assembled and on-site with a few days of its diagnosis – thanks to an international network formed for just that purpose.

Is the global health response a health innovation? Or is it an adaptation of an innovation in emergency response methods developed to deal with oil spills, or does it build on innovations developed during wartime to move wounded soldiers more quickly to effective life-saving medical treatment? We do not know the exact answer, but we do know from personal experience that in Southern Ohio, USA, emergency response teams for environmental accidents are modeled on what they have learned from studying environmental, aircraft crash, fire department, and healthcare emergency response methods. The demonstration effect of innovation in one field, as we have noted before, is powerful and is now a common way of finding new ways of doing things of use to society and the market.

The development of the ISO 9000 standard for quality management methods is a global innovation itself, in that it does not specify, as standards did in the past and still do, a hard technical standard for weights and measures of one type or another. It specifies a set of management practices that assure a basic level of quality assurance. It has been "copied" to develop a set of environmental management standards (ISO 14000) and will undoubtedly be the basis for more global management standards in the future. What ISO 9000 alone has done for global innovation is that it has facilitated the speedy global diffusion of a new set of effective management practices. This global innovation means that more firms and organizations worldwide are now able to bring variation in quality of new products and services into "control" and ready for mass production and distribution faster and at less cost than ever before.

BEST PRACTICE CASE: THE INTEGRATED RURAL DEVELOPMENT (IRD) PROGRAM IN IRELAND

The IRD program was an application of the Shared Learning process as developed by Tom Lyons, a change management developer from Dublin, Ireland.

The Shared Learning process is a collection of methods (more fully described in Chapter 6 and Chapter 8) that enables single organizations, organizations with multiple sites and up to 10 to 12 separate organizations or communities, to simultaneously plan and implement new organizational methods, strategies, or goals in a manner that enables them to adapt the ensuing innovation/change to the needs, culture, and history of each unit within a set time period and within a set budgetary limit.

The idea for the IRD program arose from discussions over the future of rural areas in the context of changes in the European Community's Common Agricultural Policy during the early 1990s.

It was thought that these changes would have negative effects on Irish rural areas generally at a time when unemployment and emigration were already very serious problems. In that context, the concept of an IRD program emerged as a means of action to promote development in rural areas.

From both the Irish Government's and the European Commission's point of view, the objective was to establish a formal process at a sub-regional level to improve employment, earning potential, quality of life, and sense of community identity among people in rural areas.

The objectives of the program were to be achieved by mobilizing local people to work for the economic, social, and cultural development of their own areas; to decide on their own development priorities; and to take the initiative to bring their goals to reality.

The emphasis was on fostering viable private and community enterprises based on full utilization of the abilities and talents of local people.

The process took 24 months and was achieved at the budget set for it. The macro-results were:

» the two-year, IRD Shared Learning™ program involving 12 communities in western Ireland resulted in 397 implemented projects (700 people involved in the planning at one point or another); and

» the 397 projects produced 600 full-time jobs, 687 part-time jobs and 1500 short-term seasonal jobs. These projects produced the equivalent of $8,700,000 per annum (1990 $ value) income for residents.

The State of the Art of

Global Innovation

» Social, political, economic issues.
» Web-related issues.
» Emergent ideas and concepts for the global innovator.
» Scouting: the simplest and most effective ongoing innovation tool.
» What are the implications of these new concepts and methods at individual and organizational level?
» A look to the future of global innovation – likely trends and developments.

The issues discussed below should not be thought of as a list of constraints only. The innovators among you will quickly see that one person's constraint or limit may well be a very large opportunity or a "design" requirement that triggers an unforeseen innovation.

SOCIAL, POLITICAL, ECONOMIC ISSUES

The Global Compact's nine principles[1] represent a substantial portion of the social, political, and economic issues which affect global innovation as the cutting edge of globalization. The principles ask world businesses to:

» support and respect the protection of internationally proclaimed human rights within their sphere of influence;
» make sure they are not complicit in human rights abuses;
» uphold freedom of association and effective recognition of the right to collective bargaining;
» promote the elimination of all forms of forced and compulsory labor;
» promote the effective abolition of child labor;
» uphold the elimination of discrimination in respect of employment and occupation;
» support a precautionary approach to environmental challenges;
» undertake initiatives to promote greater environmental responsibility; and
» encourage the development and diffusion of environmentally friendly technologies.

The World Trade Organization's (WTO) meetings at different venues around the world over the last few years have been regularly posed these questions by WTO members, by non-governmental organization (NGO) advocacy groups, and by coalitions of political activists. The same general questions (with hundreds of specific issues) have been and are being asked of the World Bank, the International Monetary Fund (IMF), agencies of the United Nations, and national governments around the globe, as well as agencies, departments, and bureaus of those national governments.

At times, the impact on a global innovation is direct. For example, when Microsoft wants to introduce a new business agreement, application, or service, its home government, as well as one or more European

Union (EU) Directorates, can ask or require significant changes, or even proscribe the actions proposed by Microsoft.

At other times, the impact of these issues is somewhat less direct but the impact may be no less important. For example, when Nike is negotiating agreements with contractors in several different countries to supply materials and/or carry out sub-assembly or final assembly of one of its apparel products, or sell its finished goods, it must take into consideration the labor laws and practices as well as the potential environmental impacts of its proposed business in each country.

This collection of issues is certainly what leads Nike's CEO Philip Knight to support clarity and global uniformity (predictability) in such standards. Knight says: "... an internationally recognized set of generally accepted social accounting principles and monitoring organizations certified to measure performance would bring greater clarity to the impact of globalization and the performance of any one company."[2]

WEB-RELATED ISSUES

We have noted earlier that the "global" impact of a global innovation is the expectation or model it creates for consumers. A feature or way of doing things in one technology, product, or service sets a standard for other technologies, products, and services. The Web is having that kind of impact, so much so that whether you are a dot.com or a bricks-and-mortar business, it (the Web) is creating expectations/standards for you and your business.

The Web's impact on globalization and global innovation has already been beyond what many might have supposed when first introduced. We can all agree that in a very few years it has radically altered:

» the quantity and quality of information now readily accessible that can be "mined" and then juxtaposed and transformed into knowledge by anyone around the globe who has access to a computer which is hooked up to the Internet – and on a 24-hours-a-day, seven-days-a-week basis;

» the ability of consumers to search for products and services for sale, as well as products and services that are free;

» the ability of companies to gather information about consumers and to reach consumers;
» the constraints of time and distance in obtaining information, products, and services; and
» the constraints of time and distance on communicating (by sound, writing, still or animated pictures, and video) with other people for a nearly infinite range of purposes in real time, or via a variety of electronic mail services.

Design characteristics of the Web

Tim Berners-Lee, the initial designer and producer of the Web, noted in a 1999 talk[3] some design characteristics of the Web that, in this context, will have an ongoing impact on global innovation similar to the nine principles of the Global Compact. We will note what Berners-Lee comments and then note how it applies to global innovation. (Berners-Lee, due to his leadership and participation in the World Wide Web Consortium has, and will continue to have, tremendous influence on the future direction of the Web and its attendant technologies.)

"It was important that it should be independent of software. It's very important that any program can talk the World Wide Web protocols (HTTP, HTML, . . .)"

Tim Berners-Lee

This relates to what amounts to being a principle for global innovation/innovators: accessibility or open architecture of your organization/product/service may/can enhance the long-term success of your innovation more than the closed or proprietary architecture favored by traditional capital- or profit-based companies.

"It's very important to be independent of the way you actually happen to access this information. It should also work if you need to have [it] read to you, because you're visually impaired or you're driving. Twenty percent of the people who [now] have access to the Web have some sort of impairment . . . So it's very important that we separate the content from the way we're presenting it."

Tim Berners-Lee

Nearly everyone talks about the importance of niche marketing as a "basic" for global innovation in the age of the Web. At the same time, however, people with what has been defined as a disability or a handicap still find themselves arguing/lobbying with business and government about improving access or usability of almost every type of product, service, or means of employment. And as the Baby Boomers of the 1950s and 1960s reach ages 60 and 70, these access issues will be no less important.

WHO'S BLIND, OR NOT SEEING CLEARLY HERE?

Low or no vision is just one disability that, under historic conditions, has limited the access of people to information, employment, transportation, etc. Laws and regulations that require improved access to products, services, education, and employment for vision-impaired people "may" be thought of as a limitation to global innovation. Putting aside natural empathy for a moment, from a strictly business point of view, once you know that there are 180 million visually impaired people in the world,[4] shouldn't you be thinking how to serve them better or create the global innovation that makes them potential customers?

"It's important that the Web should be independent of language and culture."

Tim Berners-Lee

This next point is also related to accessibility but more clearly–the most basic requirement for global innovators and innovations is that they not be limited or restricted by language or cultural barriers. If there isn't a book on the Greatest Cultural and Language Business Bloopers (or Gaffes), there ought to be - and it should be required reading for MBA students and anyone being considered for CEO or head of marketing.

"It's very important that we use . . . human intuitive ability, because everything else we can automate"

Tim Berners-Lee

Berners-Lee was referring to the human intuitive act or innovative act that takes place "When people browse across the Web and see something expressed in natural language . . . and suddenly solve a totally unrelated problem due to the incredible ability that the human brain has to spot a pattern totally out of context by a huge amount of parallel processing . . ."

Many people have had this experience on their own. It is closely related to both the accessibility and open architecture points. The questions or issues that impact global innovation are the following.

» *What would the result be if customers or potential customers could "browse" through your organization's "idea factory"?* A few software producers (too few), and a large number of e-zines, ask customers/users to write down or talk about what improvements could be made to their products, or what features they would like to see. The latest version of the Web browser, Opera, is being constructed in large part with beta-user input. Linux, the operating system alternative to Windows and Macintosh's OS X, is literally built, re-built, and expanded based on its being "open" in a number of different ways.

» *How much more innovation would come out of your organization if your employees could "browse" through the information already in your organization and could build, as well as edit, ideas in organizationally public space?* If your organizational culture inhibits that kind of activity, you are in trouble and missing a lot of potentially good ideas. If you have not structured your information technology to enable you to do this, you should. It was this type of interaction or intercreativity that inspired Berners-Lee and those working with him to create the Web in the first place.

EMERGENT IDEAS AND CONCEPTS FOR THE GLOBAL INNOVATOR

Ultimately global innovation is about people, not technology

The emergent theories, concepts, and approaches to organizing for and supporting innovation were developed during a period roughly covering 1948 to 1979. Just as the new science of quantum physics took nearly 30 years to "rush" into application due to society wanting a practical application - nuclear weapons (Einstein's General Theory of Relativity was developed in 1915) - so the "new science" of how to best organize work for innovation and active adaptation to fast-changing commercial, social, and political environments has not come into its own until organizations begin to see that the marketplace is not going to become less turbulent. If anything it will continue at its present turbulence or increase as more and more societies actively enter the global economy with goods and services higher on the value chain than raw materials, aiming to do more than serve as "back lot" assembly locations.

An obvious question is why are these ideas and methods coming into their own now and not earlier? During the 1950s and 1960s, due to the devastation of World War II, the US essentially had "world monopolies" in its booming internal market and in the international markets. At the same time, Europe and Asia were recovering from being the theatre of that war.

During the 1970s and up to the early 1980s, US companies, consumers, and government perhaps discounted the loss of internal and external market share in consumer electronics, timepieces, and cameras to lower labor cost advantages or an interest in European "style." It was only after US steel companies and auto-makers "discovered" that quality and innovation were major causes of them losing market share that they began to investigate new ways of organizing and structuring work. Quality was the first area addressed, innovation and adaptability is the new frontier. Now it seems that companies in Europe, Asia, the Pacific Rim, and North America are beginning to realize that "monopolies" gained through technological innovation will be short-lived, as more and more societies have population with sufficient skills and education to duplicate the technology and improve upon it. It is dawning on more and more people that they need more than the latest technology.

The "new science" of organizing innovation

During the early 1950s the Tavistock Institute in the United Kingdom sent researchers to investigate ways to improve productivity in Britain's coal mines. The result was that one of the researchers, Fred Emery, began a lifelong study into the conditions under which people best organized and performed purposeful work. Out of his work and that of British, Norwegian, Dutch, American, and Australian colleagues, as well that of as his wife and co-researcher Merrelyn, the Search Conference (see Chapter 10) and the Participative Design Workshop (see Chapter 7) were developed as the world's leading ways for organizations to actively adapt (innovate) to changes in the social/economic/political/physical environment and to organize/design work that is both productive and meaningful to those involved in the work. Researchers in this area have been documenting and refining their methods for some 30-plus years now. Merrelyn Emery developed the Participative Design Workshop in 1971 as a means to enable organizations to design work to meet what she and others found to be the six critical requirements for effective work. Effective work in their terms includes the ability of work groups to adapt and innovate to meet and overcome changes in their work environment. She and Fred Emery also refined the Search Conference as a means to enable whole organizations or sub-units to adapt and innovate in turbulent systems.

The six critical human requirements for effective work

1 *Adequate elbow room for decision making*. The sense that people can influence their own work and that, with the exception of specific circumstances, they don't have to ask permission for everything. Enough elbow room to feel empowered but not so much that they do not know what to do.

2 *Opportunity to learn continually on the job*. Such learning is possible when people can set goals that are reasonable challenges for them and get timely feedback on results.

3 *An optimum level of variety*. Through the avoidance of boredom and fatigue, people can gain the best advantages from settling into a satisfying and effective rhythm of work.

4 *Mutual support and respect*. Conditions where people can and do get help and respect from their co-workers.

5 *Meaningfulness*. A sense of one's own work meaningfully contributing to society. Also, to have knowledge of the whole product or

service. Many jobs lack meaningfulness, because workers see only such a small part of the final product that meaning is denied to them.

6 *A desirable future*. Put simply, not a dead-end job, but one with a career path that will allow personal growth and an increase in skills.

As it turns out, their work (the six requirements) also covers significant enhancers to learning researched by Csikszentmihalyi and Karasek.

Flow

Researcher Mihalyi Csikszentmihalyi began collecting observations on the conditions under which people were most creative, learned best, or performed at their peak in the early 1960s while at the University of Chicago (he is now at the Claremont Graduate School). His best-known work, *Flow*,[5] was published in 1990.

The essential components or conditions for flow are:

1 clear goals;
2 immediate feedback;
3 challenges that match skills; and
4 areas where action and awareness merge (work, play, performance, problem solving).

The flow diagram in Fig. 6.1 illustrates the area within which learning and innovation do occur and are more likely to occur.

Healthy work

Dr Robert Karasek, a specialist in the psychosocial aspects of work and work redesign processes, is a professor and co-director of the Lorin E. Kerr Ergonomics Institute for Occupational Injury Prevention, Massachusetts Institute of Technology. Writing in 1979, he says that work stress and the resulting physical and mental health effects, are the result of the "joint effects of the demands of a work situation and the range of decision-making freedom (discretion) available to the worker facing those demands ... Job strain occurs when job demands are high and job decision latitude is low." The "job strain" model (see Fig. 6.2[6]) states that the combination of high job demands and low job decision latitude will lead to negative physical health outcomes such as hypertension and cardiovascular disease (CVD).

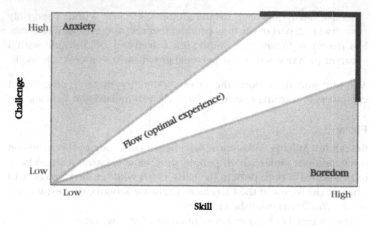

Fig. 6.1 Illustration of "flow."

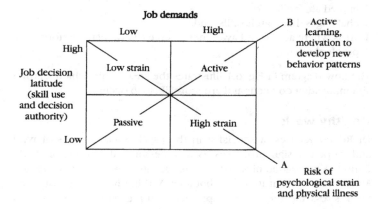

Fig. 6.2 Karasek job strain model.

One can readily see how the factors that increase learning and innovation on the one hand and reduce health risks on the other are both contained within the six requirements for effective work that were developed by the Emerys and their colleagues. Microsoft has benefited greatly from using the Search Conference in repositioning itself to meet the demands/opportunities of the Web. Syncrud, the Canadian consortium that makes synthetic oil and additives, has used the Participative Design Workshop to great advantage.

What struck you when looking at this material may well be what drew us to it as well. Many firms during their start-up or exploratory stages exhibit or "naturally" use or stress many of the six requirements for effective work. The catch seems to have been that when they grow or decide that their need for predictability is greater than their need for adaptation and change, these practices are eliminated or downplayed.

Hewlett Packard in a mid-1980s videotape admits to doing just that. During the 1980s and 90s, HP used quality teams as a means to get back a good deal of the vitality and participativeness of their early start-up days. A number of their units now use both the Search Conference and the Participative Design Workshop to support innovation and reposition units to meet new strategic needs.

SCOUTING: THE SIMPLEST AND MOST EFFECTIVE ONGOING INNOVATION TOOL

Organizing and structuring work for innovation is a major first step in supporting adaptability and the ability to innovate. Scouting, along with the Search Conference (see Chapter 10), and using the Innovation Cycle as a guide (see Chapter 8), are the other steps that will help you become more innovative.

Scouting begins with characterizing its purpose(s)

Scouting is multi-dimensional scanning to identify emergent elements that have future implications for an organization. These elements include technologies, lifestyles, and cultural trends. Macro-scouting also involves seeking to understand potential relationships amongst these elements and imaging what might develop from their interactions. Macro-scouting is illustrated by Steve Barnett's book, *The Nissan Report*,[7] which presents a series of dialogues within a group composed of people with different perspectives and disciplines on a variety of topics that are changing the nature of Nissan's environment and future. NEC has a committee composed of middle managers and executives who scout a variety of marketing and technological data to discover new product concepts. As a result, NEC has expanded its core technologies from 27 to 34. Marvin Traub, former chairman of Bloomingdale's, created the firm's vision and then used scouting teams to discover new products and to create events to support it.

Scouting can also be purposed by change agents seeking to call into question executive assumptions and beliefs. Hal Tragash, who spearheaded Xerox's quality and employee involvement effort, scouted other firms and conferences to educate himself. Next, he conducted scouting trips to unfreeze "cement-brained" Xerox managers and executives, some of whom thought Tragash was advocating Communism.

Scouting can be formal and informal

Tragash's scouting is an informal example. He initiated scouting on his own. It was not directed or designed with Xerox executives. These trips were transformed, later, into Xerox benchmarking

Great Plains Software has used a formally designed scouting system. Executives have been purposeful in designing its scouting system. Through customers and partners, Great Plains is playing with 10,000 to 15,000 active suggestions at any given time. Customer and partner surveys, user groups, and scouting customers create this information. This information is used to develop new products and improve existing ones. Associates and managers are supported in continuously transforming their operations based on this information.

The data used and information selected is dependent on scouting's purpose

Discovering new products and creating new market can involve different information sources, as illustrated by the Xerox copier and the Macintosh. A few scouting sources to consider:

» Web databases;
» organizational databases;
» observation;
» newspapers;

» publications and journals;
» e-mail lists;
» trade and professional associations;
» people's tactical knowledge;
» plant tours;
» Web chatrooms;
» conferences;
» conference papers and proceedings;
» peer interactions and networks; and
» external and internal surveys.

Take Matsushita Company's home bread-making machine, for example. After conventional methods were unable to produce a high quality bread maker, an associate suggested that she study with the head baker at a hotel famous for their bread. She learned that the baker twisted the bread in a certain way. This information was used to develop a mechanism that produced this effect.

Scouting structures evolve from the organization

Scouting structures express the creative spirit of members, the problems and opportunities they face. They may include a team, networks, outposts, scouting enterprises, or the whole organization. They may be part-time or full-time. The following are selected examples of scouting structures.

» *Team scouting.* Team scouting is illustrated by the Apple group that discovered the Macintosh while touring PARC. Apple scouting teams also discovered desktop publishing from touring customers.
» *Scouting networks.* Ken Dychtwald, CEO of Age Wave, has created an informal network of people who send him articles. He also asked them to recommend their favorite books.
» *Scouting outposts.* Yamaha's London "listening post." Associates work with leading-edge musicians to explore the future of music.
» *Scouting enterprises.* Neurobiological Technology, Inc. (NTI) is a geographically disperse network of 25 scientists who scout for promising research.

Assessing scouting findings, preparing materials, and disseminating them

There are numerous processes for assessing, preparing, disseminating, and acting upon scouting findings. Northern Telecom's scouting teams made presentations, prepared videos, and wrote reports that were circulated throughout the firm.

The US Army has a permanent unit, Center for Lessons Learned (CALL), for collecting and disseminating knowledge created. CALL teams collect event and mission information, and transform it into knowledge. When forces face uncertainty and new missions, CALL teams, for example, push useful knowledge to them. They also develop "lessons learned libraries" that can be accessed by commanders and planners.

WHAT ARE THE IMPLICATIONS OF THESE NEW CONCEPTS AND METHODS AT INDIVIDUAL AND ORGANIZATIONAL LEVEL?

The individual

If life and work seem filled with too much change, too fast, and make you uncomfortable, take heart: at least you are not alone – the last 10 years have made a lot of people feel this way and the next 10 won't make you feel any better.

If life and work seem to be a constant struggle to get new ideas accepted, to get your innovation through the web of people, interests, and regulations to the intended – or waiting – market, and you're impatient waiting for the "next thing," take heart – the last 10 years have made a lot of people feel this way and the next 10 won't make you feel any better.

The first strategy for either of the individuals above to follow is to go into business with the person who is not like you, or at least seek this person out as an innovation partner. In the process of "driving each other crazy" you are more likely to come up with innovative products and services that will be quickly accepted by the market – and perhaps in learning to better understand these two perspectives, you will be less likely to get trapped by never changing or changing too fast. A cautionary note: the objective is not to find a balance or expect one. The objective is to keep moving using the tension and variation between the two perspectives as a means to stay fresh and not drive over a cliff.

The second strategy is to figure out how to structure your work and that of those you work with so that it most closely fulfills your needs along each of the six requirements for effective work. If you do not have complete discretion over these factors, then negotiate, or find some place that agrees with you. Good knowledge-workers will not be in less demand – ever – so the probability for a favorable outcome in individual or group negotiation is better than 50%. Research shows that when these requirements are better met, both the individual and the organization benefit:

» employees are learning and innovating because they are intrinsically motivated and organizationally rewarded/recognized, and this results in profitable innovation for both the organization and the individual; and

» employees run a lower risk of cardiovascular problems and the company's healthcare costs go down.

If these two outcomes are of no interest to your employer, board, or investors, what are you waiting for? There are more and more companies looking for self-motivated, innovative people than ever before.

The organization

Jonas Ridderstråle, an assistant professor at the Centre for Advanced Studies in Leadership at the Stockholm School of Economics and co-author of *Funky Business*,[8] says: "People now control the most critical resources ... their own brains. What is crucial at many firms is perhaps not so much the core competencies as the '*core competents*' – individuals who make competencies happen. Competents are "mobile monopolies" who will stay only as long as the organization offers them something they want. To thrive, companies need to apply strategies that revolve around simultaneously attracting and reducing the power of competent individuals – talent transfusion and transformation."

A LOOK TO THE FUTURE OF GLOBAL INNOVATION – LIKELY TRENDS AND DEVELOPMENTS

Increasingly global

Developing societies in South Asia and Africa may not have what we see as being the necessary modern infrastructures to create and launch global innovations but the numbers of college educated are growing rapidly. In Uganda and Zimbabwe, the lack of a highly developed telecommunications infrastructure is being overcome by people rapidly adopting 3G cellphones and by innovative companies there who are rounding up last year's Nokia models in Europe and selling them to thrifty, phone-hungry customers.

It won't be linear, neat, or predictable

Who would have thought that bundling cosmetic surgery with safaris would be a new business that would be attractive to thrifty, sensitive, but slightly adventurous Britons? Will India be the next big pharmaceutical player, based, perhaps, on developing treatments from as yet undiscovered plants in South Asia and nearby areas? Will Russia change course and invest its oil revenue in developing itself into a software and computer powerhouse? Will a group of less developed nations opt out of existing intellectual patent and copyright conventions, or begin their own regime?

I'm a niche, you're a niche

The last two decades of splintering or niching of the mass entertainment and news media was the forerunner for the ultimate niche driver – the Web. To the unwary or unbending company, it will not take long for them to lose market share, or miss a market that they did not see. The cosmetic surgery/safari business is an example. Rural customers and blind customers, as we have noted, are being overlooked as valued customers for high-quality, high-value goods and services.

However, as niches increase and niching grows in importance, opportunities to reinvent the one-size-fits-all product will also increase. Computers and the software that accompanies it have been designed to meet the needs of business and, to a degree, students. Is there a market for relatively simple-to-operate computers and software? Think back to Microsoft Word 3.0. Is there a market for a word processing program that simple, or perhaps one with even fewer bells and whistles – for $5 or $10?

We may be biased, but we believe there is still a huge market for an automobile that meets modern safety, fuel, and environmental standards but is as easy to operate and maintain as the old Fiat 124, or even Ford's 1960s Falcon. Is the revival of the Mini just a fluke or a hint of a global need waiting to be met?

I/we want more input into your innovation

Demands for increased individual and community input/participation in commercial and political decision making will not decline, and they will not be linear, neat, or predictable.

The nine principles of the Global Compact and those design aspects of the Web will grow in importance over time.

If you want to see one plausible future of how products and services might be organized or created, take a long look at how the World Wide Web Consortium works and the principles it uses to develop "product."

We would also suggest that you listen to and take to heart the following advice from the funky guys. Nordström and Ridderstråle say: "Traditional competitive strategies will get you nowhere. Momentarily you may be one step ahead, but the others will soon catch up. The answer lies in developing a sensational strategy, embracing our emotions, and capturing our attention. Don't try to run faster – play a different game."

NOTES

1 More on the UN Secretary-General's Global Compact in the Chapter 1. The principles are drawn from the Universal Declaration of Human Rights, the ILO's Fundamental Principles on Rights at Work, and the Rio Principles on Environment and Development.

2 Philip Knight, speaking at the United Nations, New York (July 26, 2000), http://www.nikebiz.com/media/n_compact.shtml/.

3 Source: LCS 35th Anniversary celebrations, Cambridge, Massachusetts, April 4, 1999.
4 The World Health Organization (WHO) estimated in 2001 that there were 180 million persons worldwide who were visually impaired. Of these, between 40 and 45 million persons were blind. The WHO also estimates that the number of blind people worldwide is increasing by up to 2 million per year.
5 Csikszentmihalyi, M. (1990) *Flow*. Harper & Row, New York.
6 Schnall, P.L., Landsbergis, P.A., & Baker, D. (1994) "Job Strain and Cardiovascular Disease." *Annual Review of Public Health*, **15**, 381–411. See http://www.workhealth.org/strain/briefintro.html.
7 Barnett, S. (1992) *The Nissan Report*. Doubleday, New York.
8 Ridderstråle, J. & Nordström, K. (2000) *Funky Business: talent makes capital dance*. ft.com, London.

Global Innovation in Practice: Case Studies

» US, Europe, Japan, and Hong Kong – a Motorola Search Conference.
» Australia – Cyclone Hardware P&N Tools.
» India – Hindustan Lever.

Each of the following case studies represents a "timeless" set of best practices during a specific slice of time. (The practices and methods discussed may or may not be representative of present practices in the organization.) Each demonstrates the potential benefits for your organization of applying the tools or methods discussed to your particular mix of employees, customers, and suppliers, under existing market or societal conditions.

US, EUROPE, JAPAN, AND HONG KONG – A MOTOROLA SEARCH CONFERENCE

» *Time-line*: two-and-a-half days.

The Search Conference is in itself a global innovation in strategic planning. Its design enables organizations to quickly scan their environment, bring together people from around the organization who have the knowledge, skills, and experience needed to produce a breakthrough and to follow up on it, produce "out of the box" innovative thinking, devise strategies/breakthroughs, and assign work for implementation. The time-frame of the Search Conference itself is usually two-and-a-half days.

» *Preparation*: selecting the participants and gathering necessary data may take from two weeks to two months – depending on the time pressure and complexity of the issues at hand. The number of participants is usually no fewer than 12–15 and no more than 30.

The Search Conference's ability to support strategic breakthroughs or global innovation is illustrated in Microsoft's reversing itself after CEO Bill Gates discovered that the Web was more important to the company's future than originally thought. During 1995/6 and into 1997 Netscape was the clear leader in the Web browser competition. To respond to this challenge, Microsoft quietly held a series of 14 Search Conferences during 1996/7 as part of its strategic redesign efforts, while still producing existing products. By 1998/9, Microsoft moved into worldwide leadership in the Web browser competition.

The Motorola case is presented here to illustrate how the Search Conference method might be used to bring different parts of an organization together to produce a breakthrough for the whole. It is not much of a stretch to see how it could be used to improve and facilitate a better merger of two firms or create and integrate the activities and efforts of a virtual partnership or alliance. A complete run through of a Search Conference is used in Chapter 10 as part of the 10 steps to global innovation.

A QUICK OVERVIEW OF THE SEARCH CONFERENCE

As an intensive, participative process the Search Conference:

» provides a strategic framework within which other improvement strategies, such as benchmarking, value-adding partnerships, etc. can be integrated and aligned with the system's overall strategic objectives;

» explores changing market conditions so that the plan developed reflects, and is responsive to, the changing environment;

» involves a significant number (20 to 40) of leaders from the organization in developing and executing the plan for becoming an adaptive organization;

» is a two-and-a-half day off-site event in which the leadership group creates a future to which they are committed and will work for; and

» is designed for open and equal participation, regardless of hierarchy or position.

The principal advantages of the Search Conference are that:

» it produces a practical plan;

» it engenders a deep emotional and intellectual commitment to making that plan a reality;

» it effects an enduring change in the organization;

» it incorporates the deepest ideals of individuals who make up the enterprise into the plan and the planning process;

» it makes the enterprise less dependent on outside planning assistance and more self-reliant in its strategic planning and implementation; and

» it drives a proactive approach to continuous learning and adaptation into the very heart of the enterprise.

A successful search is a function of three components:

» preparation and planning;
» search conference; and
» implementation.

The Motorola Mini-Chip[1] operation's search for its future[2]

The new director of the Mini-Chip operation decided to hold a worldwide strategic planning event to learn about and better understand his business. The business had begun in the early 1990s (manufacturing capability was built in Europe, the US, Japan, and the Far East).

THE SEARCH CONFERENCE DESIGN AND TIME-LINE FOR MOTOROLA'S MINI-CHIP UNIT

Day 1 – PM

» The world around us.
» Desirable and most probable futures.

Day 2 – AM

» Where do we come from (our history)?
» What do we keep, throw out, or create?

Day 2 – PM

» Create our desirable future for 1999.
» Analyze the constraints.
» Develop strategies to overcome constraints.

Day 3 – AM
» Is desirable future still desirable?
» Action planning by self-managed teams composed of volunteers.

Twenty-five key personnel from the US, Europe, Japan, and Hong Kong gathered in Tokyo for three days in January 1995 to create their future. They would leave the event with each being part of a self-managing team responsible for involving others and keeping implementation on track.

The search begins. At 3.00 p.m. the design of the Search Conference as well as the basic concepts embedded in the design were shared with the participants. The managers of the Search Conference reviewed the nature of the search with the participants and then they moved into documenting their external environment.

The world around us

As a large group, everyone sat in a semicircle. They were asked, "What has happened in the world during the last three to five years that is novel and significant?"

A sampling of their comments:

» reduction of the US military budget;
» the GATT treaty;
» semiconductor focus;
» NAFTA;
» European Union has got bigger;
» PCS auctions (selling spectrums not allocated);
» wireless growth and acceptance by consumer;
» Asian market is now the consumer market;
» US is becoming a service economy;
» wealth redistribution is occurring globally;
» access to Internet by all;
» deregulation in Japan;
» quality is now a given to compete;
» computer-aided designs;

» consumers reject errors in high tech; and
» breakup of Soviet Union.

Desirable and most probable futures

Next, sub-groups work on desirable and probable futures for the world. The desirable world taps into their ideals but must be achievable by 1999. Their desirable future includes:

» a solution for cancer and AIDS;
» more global free trade;
» higher growth in energy conservation and recycling;
» a shorter working week; and
» a worldwide PCS boom.

Their probable future of the world tends to reflect their industry context:

» expansion and diversification of wireless technology and markets;
» developing countries' economic growth will result in improved living standards and further democratization;
» regional economic alliance will result in a shift in market shares/ manufacturing bases globally;
» wireless technology will evolve – allowing a phone number and communication tool to travel/move with an individual; and
» higher degrees of system-level integration will develop in the personal communication arena.

Remembering history

The next morning, they were unsettled by news of the Kobe earthquake. The damage and death toll, they learned, was huge; they are again reminded of the uncertainty of the environment they all share.

A circle is formed and those with the most years with Mini-Chip are asked to talk about the unit's history. After they begin, others add their voices. For the next hour the stories people tell bring the group's history to life. A time-line of formative events emerges. The newest people listen in rapt attention. It is obvious that significant obstacles were faced 10 years ago:

» there were many false starts; their own organizational father wouldn't support their independence but an internal customer did and funded their birth;

» the dirty dozen found office space and the business became a reality; and

» with pride, one person recalled the day the then CEO of Motorola called their little division "the king's jewels" upon which the future of the whole company rested.

Telling all the events, their details and relations brings out the rich context behind their work. As the time-line approaches the present, more members become involved in putting the story together and a complex web of interdependencies is woven through different experiences. One participant reported: "There is a lot we must maintain if we are to preserve who we are and the competencies we have in place."

With both the future of the world and the organization's past contexts in place, there is sufficient trust in the room to move to a weighing of the organization's weaknesses and strengths.

What do we keep, throw out, or create?

As a large group, they explore three questions simultaneously.

» What do we want to keep?
» What do we want to throw away?
» What do we need to create or invent?

What do we want to keep? Below is a sampling of what worked, what they were proud of and wanted to keep.

» The small group, team environment in product development.
» Our tenacity, benchmarking, and worldwide job rotation.
» Strong credibility with our customers.
» Our current mission is clear and appropriate.
» Our project planning abilities are a strength.

What do we want to throw away?

» The strategic business unit boundaries.
» Wafer costs are too high for one product.
» There are internal conflicts around products and people.

» Back-end reliability is inadequate.
» The research and development approach for a product group needs improvement.

What do we need to create or invent?

» We want to create worldwide centers of excellence for systems solutions and define wafer technology platforms.
» We need to enter a new market and gain more regional autonomy and funding.

What do we want to add?

» We want new ways to listen to customers and markets.
» We want to reduce cycle time for new product introductions and partner with customers.
» Let's have leadership shift to the regions in product development so we can eliminate redundancies across regions.

Creating a desirable future

Mini-Chip requires a well-defined, desirable future, expressed in six to eight strategic goals.

Four groups form to work together and create the operation's desirable future for 1999. Each group must describe the desirable future in no more than seven points. Scenarios may include a definition of market, applications, new technologies, new products, new platforms, organizational structure, business size, etc. They work for several hours and report their scenarios.

The goals for the desirable future of the Mini-Chip operation for 1999 are a stretch.

» We will have the largest portion of the worldwide market, which means we must grow faster than the market. Specific market and product figures are identified to get us there. We will participate in at least one emerging market/application.
» Worldwide centers of excellence will exist for marketing applications, design and development, manufacturing and global teamwork.
» We will drive the semiconductor, packaging, and assembly/test technology platforms and have guaranteed access to them.

» A systems-solution approach and key customer partnerships will be in place.
» Development and manufacturing cycle time will be reduced and give us a key competitive edge (seven days from order to customer's dock).
» Quality and reliability will be greater than Six Sigma and qualification cycles will disappear.

After integration of the work, all members felt committed to that desirable future and said they were prepared to make it happen.

WHAT HAPPENS WHEN TOO MANY GOALS ARE IDENTIFIED?

In cases where there are more goals than can be comfortably managed, the number must be reduced by integrating those which have strong interrelationships and/or by using a prioritization process.

What are the constraints?

In this session the group identified constraints on their desirable future and then developed strategies to overcome them. Since Mini-Chip is a relatively small unit within Motorola, a significant part of its immediate environment is the rest of the company. Four newly configured sub-groups brainstormed constraints on achieving Mini-Chip's desirable future (these were then presented by each group). The final list had two clusters of constraints.

External constraints include:

» defense spending cuts;
» strategy limited by competitors' strategies, and Motorola's equipment market share;
» the degree of acceptance both of their products and of the wireless system by customers; and
» a lot of as yet unrealized market formation with forces such as political situations, trade barriers, tariffs, and the situation in China/Asia acting as barriers.

Internal constraints include:

» organizational structure issues that limit the ability to provide systems solutions, technology availability from R&D, capital funding, and human resource issues;
» as it will take some time to develop the centers of excellence, they say they need to considerably improve their development cycle time; and
» internal customers are resistant to allowing Mini-Chip to support external markets with advanced technologies.

Next, they choose one of the top four constraints to develop strategies to address that constraint in a small group.

Strategies to overcome the constraints

To deal with the lack of sensitivity to their technology needs by Motorola's R&D, they propose that:

» they could use outside technology – buy a competitor, build partnerships, or work with a university;
» they could fund and develop technology internally without the R&D group's involvement;
» they could find a way to utilize the technology being developed for someone else by R&D; or
» they could influence from within (skunk works) rather than going to top management.

Strategies for overcoming competitor constraints were that:

» they could hire some of their key people, duplicate their technology, buy the competitor, or form a joint venture or alliance with them;
» they could thoroughly understand their competitors' internal structure and create a history map of their evolution, understand their customer focus, benchmark their products for strategic missteps and limitations, and determine their research and development expenditures and their effectiveness; or
» they could ignore their competitors' strategy, go on their own way, pull out of that market, or invest elsewhere.

Check point: is the desirable future still desirable and achievable?

While it is rare for a group to adjust their desirable goals after putting constraints under their creative gaze, this turns out to be one of those rare instances. Instead of a five-minute discussion, the group continues on for 45 minutes. The dialogue is intense. Agreement is reached and, after the discussion, just one change is made.

Action planning

It's the final morning and the group decided to take the six richly detailed desirable future goals and form them into three clusters. They chose: technology, marketing, and organizational structure.

Participants then self-select to be on of three self-managing task forces – each of which will then develop detailed action plans (strategies and tactics) to achieve their goal. They agreed that no one leaves until they figure out:

» time parameters for each group;
» criteria for monitoring progress;
» when each group will meet again;
» how they will continue to be self-managing; and
» how to bring other organizational members into the implementation phase.

Each task force takes its flip chart and agrees to publish the action plans for the rest of the community. They arrange to hold follow-up meetings in conjunction with the division-level worldwide meetings.

KEY LESSONS/INSIGHTS

» Creating a strategic plan to support organizational innovations does not need to take months and millions of dollars. With the right people in the room – those with the needed knowledge and experience – and an advanced method, the core planning can be done in three days or less.

> » Integrating the work of widespread units (geographically speaking) to support innovation can be effectively accomplished in a short period of time.
> » Improving communication and understanding between departments, units, merging companies, or alliance partners can be achieved while simultaneously improving the organization's ability to innovate and remain adaptive to its ever-changing competitive environment.

AUSTRALIA – CYCLONE HARDWARE P&N TOOLS

Even though the Search Conference is designed to help an organization to be strategically innovative and remain adaptive to its environment, Merrelyn Emery, one of the developers of the method, says: "it is insufficient on its own to maintain adaptation in the long term."[3] To remain adaptive and innovative the organization should be adaptively organized.

This case study demonstrates how organizations may organize their work to support ongoing adaptation and innovation.

Cyclone Hardware P&N Tools manufactures products for the building and engineering industries. During the time period of the case (1994/5), economic conditions had led to employee lay-offs, four-day work weeks, and minimal capital expenditure on new technology. The workforce was approximately 160 and most employees worked a day/afternoon shift operation. Before the work redesign project there were five supervision/management levels.

The work redesign project

Management had made a commitment to empower the workforce using democratic processes. The work redesign process used at the Cyclone Hardware P&N Tools plant in central Victoria, Australia was based on the work of the Australians, Drs Fred and Merrelyn Emery.

Initially a design team was selected. It was a deep slice from the organization; to review the way work was organized from a macro perspective. A new structure was developed requiring only three levels.

Once this rudimentary structure was developed, each of the teams redesigned their work in a participative design workshop, which typically takes two to three days.

In all cases the teams stayed with the three-level structure and had no role for a first-line supervisor or lead person. A role of co-ordinator or team spokesperson was to be rotated within each team. After the teams developed their new way of working, they then had to determine how their new design would work. This task involved establishing their team goals, training requirements, career paths, when to have planning meetings, etc.

At this stage, middle management had a critical role in facilitating and transitioning the journey to team self-management.

Goal setting

The operational teams initially set goals that included output, quality, training, and working conditions. One of the self-managing teams at P&N Tools set itself the following goals, which in turn were negotiated with management:

1 build up stock levels before the Christmas shutdown;
2 reduce machine setup times by 50%;
3 reduce scrap from 1.5% to 0.5%;
4 reduce absenteeism by 50%; and
5 no more than two lost-time injuries per annum.

As this team worked on providing adequate stock cover, they realized they had 1600 hours of work ahead of them, but only a 1200 hour window within which to complete it. The team overcame this problem by producing a roster system that made better use of the machines during smoke breaks and lunch, and calling on other internal resources when available.

Spin-offs from this team's commitment to achieving required stock levels have been: better equipment utilization (a 30% improvement in three months), higher output, and reduced absenteeism.

Training requirements

One of the teams at P&N Tools determined that to effectively function as a multi-skilled team they needed the following training:

» on-the-job training for machine setup;
» job rotation for adequate back-up skills;
» team co-ordinator training;
» team first aid; and
» training in minor maintenance.

All skills were to be competency-based, the critical ones requiring assessment.

TQM/JIT training

Once multi-skilling training was completed, team members then began requesting TQM/JIT tools and techniques to reduce the cost of quality and increase output. This enabled maintenance personnel to concentrate on issues such as critical breakdowns and preventative maintenance.

At the time of writing, P&N Tools' overall performance and product demand had improved to such an extent that a third production shift had been added.

Time-line

The Participative Design Workshop, similar to the Search Conference, is typically scheduled for two-and-a-half to three days for the central work. Planning and preparing for the workshop can vary in the time required, according to the needs and schedule of the company involved. On average, no more than one week of a planning team's time is needed for planning. Follow-on work such as training may take a month or so to schedule and carry out.

KEY LESSONS/INSIGHTS

The Participative Design Workshop, itself a global innovation in work design, is designed to structure work in a way that supports flow and optimal learning, the six requirements for effective work, and reduces or prevents the type of stress that leads to greater health risks and costs to individual employees and the company. While it requires a significant change in how leaders have traditionally viewed the entry-level or first-level's ability to manage itself and make responsible, productive decisions, if adopted as an organizing method, it supports adaptive innovation throughout the whole organization and increases the probability that the organization will be able to support product or service innovation, as well as react quickly to external global innovations that impact the company.

INDIA – HINDUSTAN LEVER

Hindustan Lever Ltd. is the local subsidiary of Dutch giant Unilever, the world's largest consumer products manufacturer. Hindustan Lever's global innovation? Marketing and developing products to customers that are either neglected or thought of by many other producers as marginal customers for cheap, low quality commodity products. The lessons, or new principles, learned in its Indian market can be applied in other markets worldwide with similar socio-economic and environmental conditions.

The frontier of global innovation: rural India, where state-of-the-art companies meet the dirt road. In rural India:

» the typical family in a small town earns 4800 rupees (about $103) a year farming and from working occasionally in the city;
» most wash their clothes and bodies in nearby ponds or at community water taps; and
» if soap is used at all, it's usually whichever brand is cheapest and it's for everything: their bodies, hair, and clothing.

In the past 20 years, Hindustan Lever has created a distribution system that moves its products to every corner of India. "Everybody wants brands," argues Keki Dadiseth, 55, who is in charge of home- and personal-care products worldwide for Unilever and a director of Hindustan Lever. "And there are a lot more poor people in the world than rich people. To be a global business and to have a global market share, you have to participate in all segments." M. Venkatesh, of Hindustan Lever, says, "Rural consumers want value, not just volume."

Fast Company journalist, Rekha Balu, notes, "Even the poorest of the poor, when given a choice, can be choosy about brands. In a nation where more than one-third of rural consumers watch TV and even more visit commercial centers ... If you only have two rupees (about four cents) to spare, you want value for your money – and quality products for your children."

Hindustan Lever sells everything from soups to soaps by going wherever its customers are, whether it's the weekly cattle market or the well where village women wash their clothes. Rekha Balu notes, "Marketing well-made products to the poor isn't just a business opportunity; it is a sign of commercial respect for people whose needs are usually overlooked."

Unilever (annual revenues: $43bn) anticipates that by 2010 half of its sales will come from the developing world, up 32% from its current sales. India's rural people – 12% of the world's population – present a huge untapped market.

It's more than selling "yesterday's" products, or a cheap, lower quality product.

Hindustan Lever learned that it takes a genuinely creative company to reach the poorest of the poor when they tackled increasing sales of soaps for women's hair. India is 16% of the world's population, notes Rekha Balu, but also has 28% of the world's hair, since most Indian women maintain long hair throughout their life. As noted above, most rural Indian consumers use the same soap to wash their body, their clothes, and their hair.

The innovation choice is: do you fight the prevailing behavior – one soap for everything – or do you develop a new soap that meets all needs and does a better job on washing hair to appeal to people who want clean, healthy hair? Hindustan Lever chose to develop a new product rather than sell an additional one and try to change traditional behavior.

Hindustan Lever product developers spent a year finding the right formula – a soap that was better for hair and still performed well for other uses. Their marketers had a strong beauty brand in Breeze, a discount soap. Therefore, they called their new soap Breeze 2-in-1 to build on existing brand strength. Distribution was targeted at smaller towns and rural areas of India. Dr V.M. Naik, deputy head of Hindustan Lever's Research Laboratory in Bangalore, asked about

Hindustan Lever's approach to R&D for rural India, said: "Technology that liberated consumers before can be a constraint for new innovation . . . New products require new principles."

"Consumer insight, advertising, and product development is part of Hindustan Lever's recipe for success," notes Rekha Balu. "One-third of India's £60.6mn of shampoo sales in 2000 came from packages in rural India. Lever claims 70% of those rural sales."

Time-line for this global innovation: one year to develop a new soap product – 20 years to develop the insight, sensitivity, and creativity needed.

KEY LESSONS/INSIGHTS

» Per capita use or sales can be deceiving, especially when considering the rural market in less-developed nations or in sections of developing nations that are under-developed. Listen to Hindustan Lever's Keki Dadiseth: "Even though developing markets use small quantities per capita, their huge population means a huge amount of fabric-washing products, shampoo, and so on. And even if you make modest profit levels on that, the gross profit can be much more than in the traditional markets."

» The lesson learned by Unilever in India: going to the customer, experimenting with a variety of sales methods, and doing the R&D that it takes to offer good value and quality for money can be expanded to how one thinks about low income and poor urban markets in cities around the globe – Los Angeles, Chicago, Cincinnati, Calais, Naples, Lagos, Cape Town, Mombassa, Mexico City, Ho Chi Minh City, etc.[4]

NOTES

1 This is not the real name of the unit. This group was made up of representatives from a highly sensitive group within Motorola that was distributed worldwide. They were pulled together to see if they could find ways for these units within Motorola to adapt quicker to changes in Motorola's competitive environment and enable it to leapfrog their competition in advanced chip design and manufacturing.

2 Source: Cabana, S. & Fiero, J. (1995) "The Motorola Mini-Chip operation's search for its future ... Motorola, strategic planning and the search conference." *The Journal for Quality and Participation*, July/August.

3 Emery, M. (1994) *The Search Conference: State of the Art*. Unpublished.

4 Source: Balu, R. (2001) "Strategic Innovation: Hindustan Lever Ltd." *Fast Company*, 47 (June), 120. http://www.fastcompany.com/online/47/hindustan.html © June (2001)

Key Concepts and Thinkers

» Agility and adaptability.
» Appreciative learning/observation/innovation.
» Joel Barker.
» Creative thinking/innovative thinking/"out-of-the-box" thinking – Edward de Bono.
» Discontinuous change/innovation.
» Tom Peters.
» The Innovation Cycle.
» Intrapreneurial innovation.
» Emotional innovation, funky innovation, attitude innovation – Jonas Ridderstråle and Kjell Nordström.

"To be agile and creative . . . we must structure our companies as learning organizations."

> *Tachi Kiuchi, managing director, Mitsubishi Electric, and*
> *chairman of the Future 500*

We must operate from the design principles of complex natural systems. The principles are: feedback, differentiation, co-operation, and fit.[1]

APPRECIATIVE LEARNING/OBSERVATION/INNOVATION

Bob Holder defines appreciative learning this way and its application to innovation: "This is illustrated by T.E. Lawrence in the film *Lawrence of Arabia*. When asked what his mission was, Lawrence replies, 'To appreciate the situation.' Lawrence's attitude is one of openness and mindful curiosity towards the Arabs and their potential. Lawrence's attitude was different from his British peers who are blinded by their fixed mental maps. Lawrence's appreciation of the situation led to development of an effective strategy for using the Arab forces during World War I."

Appreciative learning and observation is also closely related to the lessons Tachi Kiuchi has learned from the rainforest, as well as, we would guess, many thousands of innovators who found either part or nearly all of their invention/innovation in observing nature.

A worker at Toyota had the job of getting into the vehicle on the assembly line to insert part of the interior system. He had to do this numerous times a day and at such an awkward angle that his back and legs ached after work each day. He wanted a new way to accomplish his task. One day he observed an octopus at an aquarium reaching into an empty shell looking for food. He thought, if I could sit on that octopus's arm, I could move in and out of the vehicle with ease. He wrote up his idea as a suggestion for Toyota's suggestion system. The result was a movable, hanging "chair" adapted from a ski-lift chair, shaped like the octopus' arm, that enabled workers to move in and out of the auto being assembled. No more aching back or legs, fewer errors/waste, and an improvement in productivity.

We have no doubt that whoever "invented" the first tumbler machine to polish ball bearings, owed part of the invention to watching stones being polished in a creek, river, or shoreline by the moving action of water rolling them over each other with a mixture of sand doing the "polishing." The inventor of Velcro says that he observed how well burrs stuck to people's clothes after a walk in the fields near his home. He then applied his observation of burrs to creating a "new way" of getting items of clothing and many other items to fasten to each other.

INNOVATION STARTER/CLUE

If you are "up against it" and need a ready source for innovation, go take a walk outside in the country or the city and carry with you the question you have with your mind open to different ways of accomplishing what you want to do or its purpose. Nature has, we don't doubt, made dozens, hundreds, perhaps thousands of different ways to do what you want to do, if you will just step back and appreciate the situation or the environment.

JOEL BARKER

Joel Barker is best known perhaps for his books and videos on paradigm thinking, but one of his most valuable tools for breaking through existing thought patterns is one he calls the Implication Wheel. It is based on an active rather than reactive stance towards unintended consequences.

To actively avoid unintended consequences or to look for opportunities that may not be visible at first glance, an adaptation or brief form of the process Barker uses is as follows.

Note on a flip chart the action or decision being made and then ask, in two or three rounds: "What might happen if we do this?" During each of these rounds, try to identify five consequences (at least two positive, two negative). After developing this tree of consequences, rate each for its probability of actually happening (using your best estimate) – plus or minus 10%, 25%, 50%, or more. Negative ratings that occur in the middle of a set of plus ratings may indicate an unexpected roadblock that can be addressed before you get there, or it could indicate a disastrous consequence that leads to rethinking your plans. And yes, it is very much a structured way of forcing yourself, or your work group, through two or three levels of "why?" or "what if?". By comparison with decision making in most organizations, that will put you two or three steps ahead on your innovation journey.

GETTING OUT-OF-THE-BOX OR OUT OF A RUT

Xerox invented the market for affordable plain paper copying. For a number of years, it was, in effect, their market – they had a 60%+ market share worldwide. They were the leading edge in 1962–70. They stayed right on that very same edge and rode it up to the late 1970s and early 1980s until they found they were losing market share to high-quality, low-cost Japanese copiers. They had ridden the leading edge until it had become a rut so deep they could not see competitors coming up alongside and passing them with improvements and innovations of their own. The Innovation Cycle, which will be described below, is a way of approaching ongoing innovation – staying out of ruts or the box that success creates.

CREATIVE THINKING/INNOVATIVE THINKING/"OUT-OF-THE-BOX" THINKING – EDWARD DE BONO

Edward de Bono, a UK-based thinker, author, and consultant, uses the term "lateral thinking" to describe his approach to creativity and innovation. He notes that natural systems/self-organizing systems set up patterns and that such patterns are usually asymmetric. "This means," de Bono says, "that we normally go along the main track without even noticing the side track. But, if – somehow – we get across to the side track then, in hindsight, the route becomes obvious. This is the basis of both humor and creativity."[2] Cutting across patterns is what he calls lateral thinking.

"In humor, the storyteller suddenly places us on the side track and immediately we can see our way back to the starting point. The punch-line serves as the bridge between the main track and the side track. With lateral thinking, however, there is no storyteller to make the jump for us. So we have to devise a practical means for cutting across the tracks. We can do this by using a combination of provocation and movement.'' Provocation and movement are needed, because people generally find one way of accomplishing a task and continue doing it. (Recall the discussion on basic human behavior and the need/drive for predictability.)

There are indeed formal ways to set up provocations. These include:

» escape;
» reversal;
» exaggeration; and
» distortion and wishful thinking.

Using such step-by-step methods, the lateral thinker can set up a provocation to provoke his or her own thinking. There is no need to wait for someone to set up a provocation.

Movement is a crucial part of lateral thinking . . . provocation without movement is useless.

There are five formal ways of getting movement.

1 Extract a principle or feature and work forwards from that.
2 Focus on the difference.
3 Look at the moment-to-moment effect of putting the idea into practice.
4 Focus on the positive aspects.
5 Figure under what circumstances would there be direct value.

The random word is the simplest of all creative techniques. You simply introduce a random word by picking a slip of paper out of a pile of slips on each of which there is a word. Try thinking of a page number in a dictionary and then thinking of a position of the word on that page (say, page 127, tenth word down). Continue to the first noun, which will then be your random word. The random word provides a new entry point and as we work back from the new entry point, we increase the chances of using patterns we would never have used if we had worked outwards from the subject area.

DISCONTINUOUS CHANGE/INNOVATION

Discontinuous change is the reconceptualizing of a product or service in one or more of six ways:

» it makes doing something much, much easier;
» it combines several tasks/functions into one operation;
» it enables you to do something that could not be done by an individual prior to its introduction;
» it greatly speeds up some processes;
» it constitutes a redefinition of beauty/style/feel/sensuality that makes the product or service much more enjoyable; and/or
» it greatly reduces cost while not sacrificing quality.

In short, continuity with the past is broken – seemingly forever and at once. If you are not familiar with the new information technologies, then think about how the VCR changed the movie industry, and then how the DVD reinvented the VCR industry. DVDs have become "the market" for films in less than 18 months. They did so by compressing the learnings gleaned from the Sony videotape versus the RCA and Kodak videodisk. DVD players were introduced and priced at levels it took video players several years to reach. On a more basic human level, think about food/eating and what the microwave did and continues to do to traditional cooking.

If we haven't given enough product examples yet, go to any store that sells recorded music and try to buy a vinyl record album. In less than two years CDs destroyed a market that had thrived and existed for at least 80 years![3]

TOM PETERS

Tom Peters has been, at one and the same time, the innovation, customer service, and quality movement's head cheerleader, missionary, critic, researcher, author, and business lecture circuit headliner in North America for more than 20 years. His approach is to examine hundreds of companies searching for who is doing what the best and being rewarded by the marketplace for doing so.

Peters extracts what he sees are key principles or themes to those successes and recommends that other companies and leaders either emulate them, or at least think about how they might apply to the company they lead or work within.

Tom Peters is dismissed by people who say he has no complete theories, exhaustive "scientifically" valid research, and that on occasion he changes his mind, or admits he was wrong. He is much admired because he finds out what people are doing that works well, is rewarded by the market, and passes along the information as fast as possible in understandable language.

What he and others – such as the *Funky Business* Swedish economists Jonas Ridderstråle and Kjell Nordström – give us are kernels, or seeds from which we can grow our own wonderful garden. A friend of ours, Amy Katz, a fine group facilitator on Cincinnati, Ohio, calls these seeds or small patterns "theories on the run." And in a turbulent, fast-moving world, perhaps theories on the run are better than no theories at all.

THE INNOVATION CYCLE

The Innovation Cycle (Fig. 8.1) is a four-phase cycle of innovation or improvement.

» *Discontinuous innovation*: Discontinuous innovation reinvents a market, product, or significant aspect of the customer transaction. Another way of thinking about it is as a market-destroying product or service, or an innovation that disrupts the environment for your competitors in what was formerly a highly competitive market.
» *Continuous improvement*: This is the type of improvement or innovation that is normally addressed in total quality management (TQM). Work teams, individuals, and task teams look for ways to continuously improve their processes or to align work process in a manner that improves productivity, service, and/or quality.
» *Breakthrough improvement*: Breakthrough improvements are those that greatly enhance an existing product or service by making it less costly, easier to use, better looking, etc.
» *Another discontinuous innovation*.

The successful organization in turbulent times will be one that manages all three types of innovation and then returns to the beginning of the

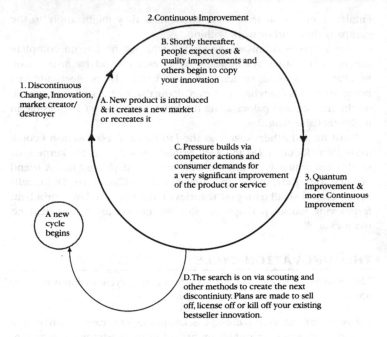

1. Discontinuous Change, Innovation, market creator/destroyer

A. New product is introduced & it creates a new market or recreates it

2. Continuous Improvement

B. Shortly thereafter, people expect cost & quality improvements and others begin to copy your innovation

C. Pressure builds via competitor actions and consumer demands for a very significant improvement of the product or service

3. Quantum Improvement & more Continuous Improvement

A new cycle begins

D. The search is on via scouting and other methods to create the next discontinuity. Plans are made to sell off, license off or kill off your existing bestseller innovation.

1. The new product/service is launched.
2. Employees (individuals and teams) begin using continuous improvement methods to improve quality, productivity and costs (TQM, Kan Ban, Poka Yok, SMED, etc.).
3. Hoshin Planning and QFD are used with teams to produce dramatic cost, quality, and/or feature and service breakthroughs. With introduction of breakthroughs, CI begins again.
4. Not long after the breakthrough introduction, ongoing scouting and innovation supporting efforts are stepped up to prepare the next market maker and breaker.

Fig. 8.1 The Innovation Cycle.

cycle so they will have a constant stream of products to serve all of their customers.

INTRAPRENEURIAL INNOVATION

"We are moving ... to organizations that engage the intelligence and creativity of all of their members. To achieve efficiency, these new kinds of work organizations count on self-directed initiative."

Gifford and Libba Pinchot

A good route to supporting innovation is enabling people to combine their ideals/integrity with work, and that is supported by increasing "choice." The Pinchots note: "Increasing choices in the workplace to more nearly resemble the choices a customer might have in an entrepreneurial marketplace can suddenly give room for people to pull off little miracles of serving others' needs."

CASE STUDY OF CHOICE – INTRAPRENEURING SUPPORTING INNOVATION

Early in the era of AIDS, The New York Blood Bank asked DuPont's Medical Products Department for help in tracking the history of every pint of blood passing through its hands. Their supplier in DuPont was the Medical Products Department, which sold blood chemistry analyzers but not computer software. The Medical Products people sought help from their departmental and corporate information technology staffs . . . but could not deliver the system anywhere near the 90-day window demanded by the customer. Medical Products people were too intrapreneurial to give up that easily. They had heard of a small information technology group within DuPont's huge fibers business that was experimenting with a new system . . . for writing software faster. IEA (Information Engineers Associates) had built a database to track the history and quality of every bobbin of Kevlar® fiber manufactured at the Fiber Department's Richmond, Virginia plant. And now the IEA people jumped at this chance to *bring their work and their integrity together*, and said they'd do the job within the deadline.

As IEA's reputation spread throughout DuPont, they were called upon again to cross bureaucratic boundaries, this time to create a database to track radiation in the ground water in the test wells around DuPont's nuclear materials production site at Savannah River. When they succeeded again in 90 days, the word spread and groups all over DuPont wanted their services. Soon IEA's success became a problem. Fibers management asked them to do less work for other departments and focus on Fibers' needs. Rather than clip their own wings, IEA went to corporate finances for help. They said, we don't want to be a staff group anymore; we want to be a profit center and live on what we can sell internally. The finance officer put on a glum face and said, "You are a staff function – you can't be a profit center." Then he winked, laughed and said, "How would you like to be a 'negative cost center'?" Their revenues exceeded their costs, and they grew to 120 employees. As the result of the systems to support free intraprise exchange, business units all over DuPont began getting better information technology service at a lower cost.

EMOTIONAL INNOVATION, FUNKY INNOVATION, ATTITUDE INNOVATION – JONAS RIDDERSTRÅLE AND KJELL NORDSTRÖM

Jonas Ridderstråle and Kjell Nordström are both located at the Stockholm School of Economics. Jonas is at the Center for Advanced Studies in Leadership and Kjell is at the Institute of International Business. They are fast becoming the "Tom Peterses" of Europe and Asia (their book *Funky Business*[4] has been published in Japan, Korea, Taiwan, and the People's Republic of China, as well as in the USA and Israel).

They note that: "Nokia and other funky firms succeed because they have realized that they need to exploit the last taboo. They need to compete on feelings and fantasy. Welcome to e(motional)-commerce. Economies of scale and skill still matter, but the new game is one of economies of soul. The only way to make real profit is to attract the emotional rather than the rational consumer. Why do emotions matter so much? Well, in a world with more than 1700 Internet banks in Europe alone, the business opportunities for Average, Inc. are pretty awful. But there are other reasons too. Research in neuroscience shows that the brain's limbic system, which governs our feelings, is way more powerful than the neocortex that controls intellect. The traffic instructions that evolution provided our brains with are pretty clear: emotions have the right of precedence. Logic just has to wait. So keep on going for the hearts, guts, and groins of people – there is even scientific evidence to back you this time."

NOTES

1 Source: a Future 500 booklet: *What I Learned in the Rain Forest.*
2 De Bono, E. (1988) "Serious Creativity: Exploring Patterns of Thought." *The Journal for Quality and Participation*, September/October.
3 Source: Ned Hamson and Bob Holder.
4 Ridderstråle, J. & Nordström, K. (2000) *Funky Business: talent makes capital dance.* ft.com, London.

Global Innovation
Resources

» Government agencies, associations, institutes, and centers.
» ISO 9000 and ISO 14000 related resources.
» Websites of publications and other organizations.
» Websites for scouting the "plus" aspects of global innovation.
» Recommended books.
» Recommended articles.

This is not a definitive listing of associations, articles, books, or Websites devoted to, or with a significant interest in, global innovation. It is a listing of organizations that we know of that offer a great deal of theory and practice-based content and an opportunity to network with experienced practitioners. That is not to say that those not listed are any less knowledgeable; only that we are not familiar enough with them to list them, nor is there sufficient room here.

GOVERNMENT AGENCIES, ASSOCIATIONS, INSTITUTES, AND CENTERS

The Association for Quality and Participation (AQP)

» http://www.aqp.org

This is an international not-for-profit membership association dedicated to improving workplaces through quality and participation practices. In 2001, it affiliated with the ASQ. The AQP has sponsored a Team Excellence Award since 1985.

The Journal for Quality and Participation is the official journal for the AQP and is a leading journal in its field. *News For A Change* is the newsletter of the AQP.

The American Society for Quality (ASQ)

» http://www.asq.org/

ASQ has been the leading quality improvement organization in the United States for more than 50 years.

Quality Progress, ASQ's flagship publication, includes in-depth articles describing the application of innovative methods in areas such as knowledge management, process improvement, and organizational behavior.

The Asian Productivity Organization

» http://www.apo-tokyo.org/

The Asian Productivity Organization was created in 1961 to oversee productivity development throughout Asia and the Pacific. Its newsletter is an excellent summary of its continuing efforts to promote innovative management practices, including its latest initiative: Green Productivity (http://www.apo-tokyo.org/gp.new/index.htm).

Best Manufacturing Practices (BMP)

» http://www.bmpcoe.org/

The BMP Center of Excellence is a partnership between the Office of Naval Research's BMP Program, the Department of Commerce's Bureau of Export Administration, and the University of Maryland's Engineering Research Center.

British Standards Institution (BSI)

» http://www.bsi-global.com/index.html

The British Standards Institution is the representative for the United Kingdom in ISO standard-making committees.

BSI's *Business Standards Magazine* is an online publication that covers all aspects of standards development and applications through news reports, interviews, and case studies: http://www.bsiamericas. com/bsi_site/bizstand/index.html.

Corporate Design Foundation (CDF)

» http://www.cdf.org

This site is the Net home of *The Journal of Business and Design*. This publication illustrates how design can be a source of innovation. It contains interviews and case studies. The site also has a resource section that includes links to design organizations, businesses, publications, and business schools.

Council for Logistics Management (CLM)

» http://www.clm1.org

This site provides resources for developing innovative value-chain business models. It contains case studies from Asian, American, and European firms.

EUREKA: a Europe-wide network for industrial R&D

» http://www3.eureka.be/Home/

Launched in 1985, EUREKA has already changed the face of pan-European co-operative research and development. It is a framework through which industry and research institutes from 31 countries and the European Union develop and exploit the technologies crucial to global competitiveness and a better quality of life.

European Foundation for Quality Management (EFQM)

» http://www.efqm.org/

The European Foundation for Quality Management was founded in 1988 by the presidents of 14 major European companies, with the endorsement of the European Commission.

European Organization for Quality (EOQ)

» http://www.eoq.org/

The European Organization for Quality is the European interdisciplinary organization striving for effective improvement in the sphere of quality management. Established in 1956, the EOQ's present membership includes 34 national European quality organizations.

European Quality is the official journal of the EOQ and is a high-level management publication focused on quality in all aspects: http://www.eoq.org/WhatIsEOQ_EuropeanQualityJournal.html.

The European Union online: EU official documents

» http://europa.eu.int/abc/off/index_en.htm

The Futures and Innovation Unit of the United Kingdom (FIU)

» http://www.innovation.gov.uk/index.html

The future for business and its relationship with society is being affected by events of a national and global nature. Teams within the FIU are working on a range of possible scenarios, visualizing the future and its possible effects. Contains many case studies of innovation.

The Global Alliance

» http://www.theglobalalliance.com/

The primary goal of the Global Alliance is to build a sustainable assessment and development process and the infrastructure to ensure it lasts.

The Global Compact

» http://www.unglobalcompact.org

The Global Compact is a uniquely positioned instrument for promoting the aims of global corporate citizenship and social responsibility. Its foundations are lodged in the UN's own values and mission, on which it is able to build additional competencies and strengths.

International Labour Organization (ILO)

» http://www.ilo.org/

The International Labour Organization is the specialized UN agency which seeks the promotion of social justice and internationally recognized human and labor rights. It was founded in 1919 and is the only surviving major creation of the Treaty of Versailles, which brought the League of Nations into being. It became the first specialized agency of the UN in 1946. Reports on the Decent Work Conference November 2, 2001 in Geneva: http://www.ilo.org/public/english/employment/geforum/index.htm.

Knowledge@Wharton

» http://knowledge.wharton.upenn.edu

Knowledge@Wharton is the Wharton Business School's site. It includes an entrepreneurship and innovation category. The site is free. However, first-time visitors need to register to access site materials and to download articles in PDF form.

MIT's "Inventing the Organizations of the 21st Century" initiative

» http://ccs.mit.edu/21c/

Thomas Malone, Peter Senge, and Thomas Kochan are co-founders. An interesting and informative white paper or manifesto in PDF format is available.

National Innovation Foundation (NIF) of India

» http://www.nifindia.org/

The Department of Science and Technology helped establish the National Innovation Foundation of India, on March 1, 2000, with the main goal of providing institutional support in scouting, spawning, sustaining, and scaling up grassroots green innovations and helping their transition to self-supporting activities.

Peter Drucker Foundation

» http://drucker.org/

The Drucker Foundation is devoted to supporting non-profit innovation. It includes online issues of *Leader To Leader*. The publication presents articles for developing and leading innovative non-profit. A free organizational assessment and publication on collaboration in PDF form are available.

QFD – Quality Function Deployment Institute

» http://www.qfdi.org/

QFD is a tool that is excellent for determining what customers want from an organization – both services and products.

Society for Competitive Intelligence

» http://www.scip.org/

The Society for Competitive Intelligence's site presents publications containing articles for those engaging in CI.

SRISTI

» http://www.sristi.org/

SRISTI is a non-governmental organization set up to strengthen the creativity of grassroots inventors, innovators, and ecopreneurs engaged in conserving biodiversity and developing eco-friendly solutions to local problems. Sponsors of the Asian Innovation Awards. Their Honey Bee Network allows you to search the biggest database on grassroots innovations and contemporary/traditional innovative practices: http://www.sristi.org/knownetgrin.html.

ISO 9000 AND ISO 14000 RELATED RESOURCES

» The American National Standards Institute is the US representative in ISO standard-making committees: http://www.ansi.org/.
» The British Standards Institution (BSI) provides expertise in product testing, CE marking, global trade inspection, environmental management, and information security, and provides technical advice to exporters: http://www.bsi-global.com/index.html.
» BSI's *Business Standards Magazine* is an online publication that covers all aspects of standards development and applications through news reports, interviews, and case studies: http://www.bsiamericas.com/bsi_site/bizstand/index.html.
» International Organization for Standardization: http://www.iso.ch/iso/en/ISOOnline.frontpage.

Based in Geneva, Switzerland, ISO is a non-governmental organization established in 1947 that promotes the development of standardization and related activities. Its newsletters can be a good source of information on updates on ISO matters. General information on the ISO 9000 standards can be found at ISO's Technical Committee no.176, Sub-committee no.2 (ISO/TC 176/SC 2): http://isotc176sc2.elysium-ltd.net/.

WEBSITES OF PUBLICATIONS AND OTHER ORGANIZATIONS

Bettermanagement

» http://www.bettermanagement.com/

Bettermanagement focuses on providing information on management and organization practices and methods that will allow a firm to produce cost-effective innovations. Resources include white papers, articles, and book reviews. The site is free. However, first-time visitors need to register to access site materials and to download articles in PDF form.

BrandChannel.com

» http://www.brandchannel.com

BrandChannel.com presents innovative branding and marketing ideas, research, and techniques. The site is free. However, first-time visitors need to register to download articles in PDF form.

Strategy and Business

» http://www.strategy-business.com/

Strategy and Business contains articles, book reviews, interviews, and numerous case studies on supporting and managing innovation. The site is free. However, first-time visitors need to register to download articles in PDF form.

Cambridge Technology Partners

» http://www.ctp.com

The site has a number of excellent works on the new economy, emerging business models, value chains, B2B commerce, knowledge management, and customer loyalty. The site is free. First-time visitors need to register to download articles in PDF form.

Center for Business Innovation

» http://www.cbi.cgey.com/

This site contains articles, tools, and research on such topics as biology and business, globalization, change management, valuing intangibles and intellectual capital, and connected business and economy. Presented materials can be downloaded.

Context

» http://www.contextmag.com

Context is a publication developed for the emerging digital age. It contains articles, book reviews, and interviews with innovative business leaders.

Fast Company

» http://www.fastcompany.com

Fast Company provides innovative ideas, management and organizational practices, and features on innovative firms and individuals. The site's articles are free. However, first-time visitors need to register to download articles in PDF form.

Global Business Council

» http://www.atkearney.com

Established in 1992, the Global Business Policy Council is a strategic service that helps chief executives monitor and capitalize on geopolitical, economic, social, and technological change worldwide. The site presents research, white papers, and case studies.

The McKinsey Quarterly

» http://www.mckinseyquarterly.com

The McKinsey Quarterly is the journal of the McKinsey consulting firm. The site is free. However, first-time visitors need to register to download articles in PDF form. The publication has numerous articles on innovation, knowledge management, and innovative organizational and managerial practices. These articles discuss innovation in North America, Asia, Russia, Western and Eastern Europe, and South America.

The McKenna Group

» http://www.regis.com

The McKenna Group presents innovative ideas and methods for discovering customer need and marketing to them. The site's articles are free. Most are in PDF form.

Tom Peters

» http://www.tompeters.com/

Peters' site contains interviews with leading business thinkers. It also includes short articles by Peters and associates. Peters' latest thoughts are present on slides that can be downloaded for free.

Pinchot and Company: Gifford and Libba Pinchot

» http://www.pinchot.com/

Intrapreneuring and innovation. A number of excellent free articles at the site.

Smartalliances.com

» http://www.smartalliances.com/

Smartalliances.com has information on developing and maintaining successful alliances. The site contains articles, books, and best practice cases.

Strategic Horizon

» http://www.customization.com

This is the Net home of Joe Pine and Jim Gilmore. Pine and Gilmore present the idea that we are not in an age of information and e-commerce but that of creating experience and transformational offerings. The site contains resources, books, and articles on experience offerings and mass customization.

Sveiby Intellectual Capital and Knowledge Management

» http://www.sveiby.com/

This site contains a large number of articles and tools for developing and implementing knowledge management, and measuring and enhancing intellectual capital.

Xerox PARC

» http://www.parc.xerox.com/sitemap.html

Xerox PARC's "letter to researchers" is an exceptional statement about the nature of business innovation. The site contains innovative ideas about the future of computing and the Net. The site's research is free. It also illustrates PARC's innovative methodology for developing "breakthrough" products.

WEBSITES FOR SCOUTING THE "PLUS" ASPECTS OF GLOBAL INNOVATION

The Club of Rome

» http://www.clubofrome.org/

The Club of Rome is a global think-tank and center of innovation and initiative. It brings together scientists, economists, businessmen, international high civil servants, heads of state, and former heads of state from all five continents, who are convinced that the future of humankind is not determined once and for all and that each human being can contribute to the improvement of societies. The papers on the Annual Conferences may be downloaded direct to your computer: http://www.clubofrome.org/archive/conferences.html.

Earthwatch Institute

» http://www.earthwatch.org/

Earthwatch Institute operates on a very simple but radical notion: that if you fully involve the general public in the process of science, you not only give them understanding, you give the world a future.

Fred Emery Institute Ltd

» http://www.fredemery.com.au

The depository and principal training site for Fred and Merrelyn Emery's work on the Search Conference and Open Systems Theory.

The Global Environment & Technology Foundation (GETF)

» http://www.getf.org/homepage.cfm

The Global Environment & Technology Foundation promotes the development and use of innovative technology to achieve sustainable development.

The World Future Society

» http://www.wfs.org/

The World Future Society is an association of people interested in how social and technological developments are shaping the future. Its primary publication *The Futurist* is a bi-monthly magazine published since 1967.

New Renaissance

» http://www.ru.org/

New Renaissance is a quarterly magazine serving as a forum for progressive discussion on the future of society.

Since 1990, it has been bringing a holistic perspective to the economic, environmental, political, social, spiritual, and cultural concerns of today. Past issues available online.

YES! A Journal of Positive Futures

» http://yesmagazine.org/index.htm

YES! A Journal of Positive Futures combines analysis of key problems with news of the actions people are taking in the United States and around the world to create a more positive future. Stories commonly report on similar actions in many places that reveal patterns that show the potential for significant social change.

RECOMMENDED BOOKS

Books that are "out of print" are now available through resale on the Internet. Amazon.com, for example, both solicits and lists used books that individuals wish to sell. Many of the Internet book sales sites also supply access to customer's own "recommended books" for innovation.

» Crosby, P.B. (1992) *Completeness, Quality for the 21st Century.* Dutton, New York.

Perhaps one of the best books for senior executives. A look at the future of success from a very high level.

» Csikszentmihalyi, M. (1990) *Flow.* Harper & Row, New York.

Flow describes the conditions that support and sustain learning and innovation.

» Csikszentmihalyi, M. (1993) *The Evolving Self.* HarperCollins, New York.

» Csikszentmihalyi, M. (1996) *Creativity: Flow and the Psychology of Discovery and Invention.* HarperCollins, New York.

» Emery, M. (1999) *Searching: The Theory and Practice of Making Cultural Change.* (Dialogues on Work and Innovation, v. 4) John Benjamins Pub. Co., Philadelphia.

» Hamel, G. & Prahalad, C.K. (1994) *Competing for the Future.* Harvard Business School Press, Boston, MA.

This is a must-read for anyone seeking to capitalize on emerging opportunities that arise with globalization, new technologies, and scientific discoveries that will unfold over the next 20–40 years.

» Hamson, N., Heckman, F., Lyons, T., Exterbille, K., & Beerten P. (1997) *After Atlantis: Working, Managing, and Leading in Turbulent Times.* Butterworth-Heinemann, Newton, MA.

Gifford Pinchot says this book will save you 10 years in figuring out how to recreate your organization to cope and compete successfully during these turbulent times.

» Karasek, R. & Theorell, T. (1990) *Healthy Work, Stress, Productivity and the Reconstruction of Working Life.* Basic Books, New York (1992 paper).

» Mizuno, S. & Akao, Y. (eds) (1994) *QFD: The Customer Driven Approach to Quality Planning and Deployment.* Asian Productivity Organization, Tokyo.

This book details quality-function deployment activities and discusses process design and quality deployment.

» Nayak, P.R. & Ketteringham, J. (1994) *Breakthroughs*. Pfeiffer, San Diego.

Breakthroughs' beauty is that the authors present the chaos and uncertainty of developing breakthrough improvements. It concludes with an insightful summary of the realities and myths about breakthroughs.

» Peters, T. (1988) *Thriving on Chaos: Handbook for a Management Revolution*. Harper & Row, New York.

» Pine, J. & Gilmore, J. (eds) (2000) *Market of One*. Harvard Business School Press, Boston.

Pine and Gilmore present a collection of articles on mass customization and one-to-one marketing. The collection begins with Peter Drucker's article on a theory of new manufacturing, in which he presents a new conceptual framework for mass customization.

» Schultz, H. & Yang, D. (1997) *Pour Your Heart Into It – How Starbucks Built a Company One Cup at a Time*. Hyperion, New York.

Pour Your Heart Into It is a testimony of the critical role of soul in innovation. Schultz presents a detailed characterization of Starbucks innovations in branding, marketing, human resources, and creating an experience.

» Senge, P.M. (1994) *The Fifth Discipline: The Art and Practice of the Learning Organization*. Currency/Doubleday, New York.

This book and Senge's center at MIT launched the "learning organization" movement.

RECOMMENDED ARTICLES

While there are literally thousands of articles available, the ones selected here are those you would want to have stored away just in case your server crashed for good or your library burned to the ground.

» Cabana, S. & Fiero, J. (1995) "The Motorola Mini-Chip operation's search for its future ... Motorola, strategic planning and the search conference." *The Journal for Quality and Participation*, July/August.

An excellent case study of how the search conference can be used for strategic planning of quality management.

» Crosby, P.B. (1992) "Getting from Here to There, 21st Century Leadership." *The Journal for Quality and Participation*, July/August.

  The essence of his book on completeness. Leadership in quality from the senior executive's view.
» Kodama, F. (1992) "Technology Fusion and the New R&D." *Harvard Business Review*, 70(4), 70–8.

  Kodama presents guidelines and principles, illustrated by detailed case examples, on engaging in fusion innovation.
» Senge, P. (1992) "The Real Message of the Quality Movement: Building Learning Organizations." *The Journal for Quality and Participation*, March/April.

  Senge synthesizes the teachings of Deming with the innovative scenario planning approach of Arie de Geus.
» Yoshihara, H. (1991) "On the March to Perfection A New Scenario for Productivity Challenges." *The Journal for Quality and Participation*, July/August.
» Wheatley, M.J. (1994) "Reinventing the 21st century Army . . . Can the US Army become a learning organization?" *The Journal for Quality and Participation*, March/April.
» De Bono, E. (1988) "Serious Creativity: Exploring Patterns of Thought." *The Journal for Quality and Participation*, September/October.
» Holder, R.J. & Hamson, N. (1995) "Innovation and the future ain't what they used to be . . . Requisite for future success . . . discontinuous improvement." *The Journal for Quality and Participation*, September/October.
» Guaspari, J. (1991) "Do You Want Me to Recreate the World or Just My Corner of It? Limits Can Be Liberating." *The Journal for Quality and Participation*, September/October.
» Holder, R. & McKinney, R. (1991) "What Have We Done To Innovation and How Can We Change? Uncaging Innovation and Scouting." *The Journal for Quality and Participation*, September/October.
» Holder, R. & McKinney, R. (1993) "Serendipity, the art of discontinuous improvement and staying alive . . . Wasn't that new just yesterday?" *The Journal for Quality and Participation*, December.

» Holder, R.J. (1992) "Clues for Experiencing a World When There Is No Path ... Corporate Change and the Hero's Quest." *The Journal for Quality and Participation*, July/August.

» Holder, R.J. (1995) "Developing scouting systems ... Creating new games through scouting." *The Journal for Quality and Participation*, January/February.

» Holder, R.J. (1995) "Of poisons, cures and insightful remedies instead of bangles, baubles and beads ... Themes for creating change in the discontinuity age." *The Journal for Quality and Participation*, July/August.

» Miller, W.C. (1995) "Four distinct strategies for quality improvement ... Is innovation built into your improvement processes?" *The Journal for Quality and Participation*, January/February.

» Fritz, R. (interviewed by Kevin McManus) (1998) "How Creativity Nurtures the Nature of Invention." *The Journal for Quality and Participation*, November/December.

» Ashkenas, R. (1998) "Real Innovation Knows No Boundaries." *The Journal for Quality and Participation*, November/December.

Ten Steps to Making it Work: Pulling it all Together

1 Scouting.
2 Determine where your organization is in its innovation cycle.
3 Adopt leadership and management methods that support ongoing high performance and adaptability.
  » The Search Conference: a compact and robust method for "getting outside of the box" and on to being globally innovative.
4 Changes in the world important into the future.
5 Trends and forces directly affecting our system.
6 Common history of our system.
7 Our current system: what to keep, throw out, create.
8 Desirable future of our system.
9 Action planning to identify goals, means to attain the desirable future.
10 Diffusion of the plan to the organization and implementing the plan.

To become an effective global innovator and sustain those efforts the following macro steps are recommended.

1. SCOUTING

Initiate ongoing scouting activities at different levels of your organization (see descriptions and resources for scouting in Chapters 2, 6, 7, 8, and 9).

2. DETERMINE WHERE YOUR ORGANIZATION IS IN ITS INNOVATION CYCLE

Are you ready to start a new cycle in some product lines, and apply continuous improvement or breakthrough improvement in others?

» If the organization does not already have a quality management process, you should design and implement one appropriate for your organization. You may well need to aim for ISO 9000 registration due to customer requirements and/or actions of competitors. *Managing Quality*, another book in the ExpressExec series, is highly recommended as a means to get started in quality management.

» If the organization does not already have an environmental quality management process, you should design and implement one appropriate for your organization. You may well need to aim for ISO 14000 registration due to customer requirements and/or actions of competitors.

» If you do not manufacture but do operate or market internationally, you should look carefully at the Global Compact, consider how it applies to your enterprise, and either join it or apply the principles appropriate for your firm. Even if you are not currently operating or marketing internationally, you should keep in mind two issues: one, that operating as if you already had an international competitor that is a member of the Global Compact will help to keep you on the cutting edge and perhaps dissuade international competitors from challenging you in your market; and two, that aligning yourself to complying with the Global Compact will prepare you for the probability that within the next 10 years there will be an international standard based on the ISO management series that will cover the non-environmental aspects of the Global Compact.

3. ADOPT LEADERSHIP AND MANAGEMENT METHODS THAT SUPPORT ONGOING HIGH PERFORMANCE AND ADAPTABILITY

Brief evolution of the Search Conference method of strategic planning

1960

» Fred Emery and Eric Trist create the first participative strategic planning method and field test it in 1960 with the Bristol Siddeley Aircraft Engine Company in Great Britain. They call the method process searching, or the search conference.

1965

» Emery and Trist publish a ground-breaking causal texture article in human relations. Their message: the environment is an entity that changes its nature over time. A change in the environment affects the systems within it in ways different from that of the previous environment.

» Bureaucratic organizations were introduced to produce a competitive advantage in a stable competitive environment whose reign is ending. These bureaucratic structures were successful and viable for a time; however, they did not meet people's critical requirements for work. The result was that people felt alienated and unsatisfied at work.

» We are in a turbulent and uncertain environment where the bureaucratic, hierarchical structures and principles are more and more out of place and dysfunctional.

» In an uncertain environment you need flexible, adaptive behavior and the capacity for the continuous redesign of work and adjustment to strategic plans.

1970s

» Fred and Merrelyn Emery elaborated upon open systems theory to strengthen the method. They conducted 300 search conferences during the 1970s in Australia. It was during this intense research and application period that the method was further developed, creating its strong theoretical base. Evolution of the method continues today through the interplay between theoretical understanding and application.

1980s

» During the early 1980s, the search was brought to Canada, and in 1982, the Emerys brought it to the US.

1993

» Fred and Merrelyn Emery began sharing their approach with practitioners at a series of seminars and conducted a search on the future of participative democracy in US, Canadian, and Mexican workplaces.

The Search Conference for strategic innovation

The Search Conference process helps organizations break through limiting assumptions and creates an environment, or "structure," that facilitates innovative learning. The following examples are just four ways you might use the search conference to support your global innovation efforts.

» Identify new ways of reaching/expanding your existing market, or markets that are not currently "visible." For example, in the US it was not until people could "see" teens, teeny-boppers, hippies, yuppies, boomers, Gen-Xers, hip-hoppers, or gangstas that they could market to them.
» Redefine an existing product or service, or perceive an opportunity or need for an entirely new product or service.
» After deciding that one-to-one customer service or customized service, for example, is lacking in your sector and would be seen as an attractive innovation, the Search Conference could be used to reorganize your organization in order to provide that service.
» It could be quite useful, in fact essential, in assisting two organizations to successfully merge, or partner, to offer or give birth to a global innovation.

Overall design of the Search Conference ...

The Search Conference resembles a funnel in its design. It begins with the widest possible perspective, then it narrows down to specific key actions, widening again as the group diffuses and implements its vision to the rest of the organizational community. It consists of the following seven distinct steps or parts.

1 *Changes in the world important into the future*.
2 *Trends and forces directly affecting our system* – This first part of the conference consists of a series of tasks to learn what's happening in the global and more direct environment. This sheds light on how the organization is, or could be, responding to environmental changes.
3 *Common history of our system* – Next the organization does an appreciative inquiry into the past, exploring its history and heritage, followed by an assessment on the current state of affairs.
4 *Our current system* – What to keep, throw out, create.
5 *Desirable future of our system* – Based on the shared information of the environment and organization itself, this part of the conference puts people before the task of developing a vision of their organization's most desirable future. The outcome is a series of agreed-upon vision statements.
6 *Action planning to identify goals; means to attain the desirable future* – In the last two steps of the Search Conference, participants turn desirable vision statements into achievable goals by anticipating potential constraints and devising strategies to get around them.
7 *Diffusion of the plan to the organization and implementing the plan* – Finally, action plans and strategies for diffusion and implementation are developed.

Background and pre-steps to the Search Conference

The Search Conference goal is to assist the enterprise in creating strategies and action plans, which will enable it to attain and maintain a flexible and proactively adaptive relationship between itself and its environment.

Tasks of top management and the conference manager

The task of top management is to bring together 20 to 40 of those people who carry the strategic knowledge of their organization.

The conference manager's task is to collaboratively design and manage the learning environment, the process, and the structure of the puzzle-solving process. Conference managers will brief the senior manager about the process and the participants' role. Out of this discussion will emerge a workable design and an understanding of who ought to participate in the conference.

Interaction between the enterprise's leader and Search Conference managers identifies research and data collection needs. For example, interviews with critical customers and a full range of the enterprise's employees on their perceptions of the task environment are often conducted. In addition, plans/decisions are made for collecting all reports, statistics, customer input, employee insights, and information about the system as it really works, and expert information relevant to your enterprise and its environment.

Search Conference code of behavior and expectations

» People are encouraged to be – and are supported for being – open with each other (no secrets, all information is available).
» To facilitate the open exchange of ideas and views, as well as creative thinking, official status differences are kept out of the conference.
» The participants are responsible for all content work and for making the plan happen. The participants are also responsible for controlling and co-ordinating their own work as a large self-managing group after the planning process. This group will then have to involve other organizational members whose abilities can contribute to making that future a reality.

The choice of participants

The selection of participants is always critical but will vary depending on the type of organization. For example, in an organization with a national or global center and a number of regional and/or out-of-country field operations, one needs to consider bringing in representatives who have knowledge, responsibility, and influence relevant to strategic planning and implementation. If the operation is very large and widespread, then one might consider holding a series of Search Conferences in the field and then holding a final search that integrates and fine tunes those already held.

4. THE SEARCH BEGINS: CHANGES IN THE WORLD IMPORTANT INTO THE FUTURE

Why focus on the external environment? Traditional strategic planning tends to assume stability and little change within the external environment's interacting systems – which is less true today than ever before. The old "Big Three" auto-makers in the US were so intent on, and used to, competing against each other, that they either failed to notice or take seriously the growing acceptance of Toyota, and then Datsun, automobiles in the California market.

Documenting the external environment

As a large group, everyone sits in a semicircle facing two clean flip charts. It is time to analyze the external environment from the global as well as your industry or sector's perspective. The question is, "What has happened in the last three to five years that is novel and significant?"

As items are mentioned, people begin to write their comments. Sample issues could include:

» the Euro is real!;
» the GATT treaty;
» the Global Compact;
» international terror;
» human rights an international issue;
» animal rights an international issue;
» women's and children's rights an international issue;
» NATO's changing role;
» European Community has got bigger;
» everyone is deregulating – increased consumer choices;
» China as a global parts supplier;
» wireless growth and acceptance by consumers;
» computers are in everything and everywhere;
» Asian market is now the consumer market;
» US is becoming a service economy;

» genetically modified foods;
» manufacturing in emerging economies is increasing;
» access to Internet by all;
» Japan still recovering from "burst bubble" economy;
» dot.com crash;
» quality is now a given to compete – ISO 9000 reigns;
» environment is becoming a given to compete – ISO 14000 is marching on!;
» computer-aided design, training, and simulations for everything!;
» lifelong learning a growth area;
» ageing of "boomers";
» healthcare and leisure industries will boom/are booming;
» healthcare uneven globally;
» HIV a global threat;
» India a major supplier of IT engineers, workers, coders; and
» multimedia interest still growing exponentially.

Defining a desirable future for the world in 2007

Next, sub-groups work on desirable and probable futures for the world. The desirable world taps into the ideals of individuals and helps to get people further "out of their corporate box" to see how they and consumers are affected by the larger systems. The goals must still be achievable by 2007 (five years out).

Their desirable future could include such goals as:

» a solution for cancer and HIV; and/or
» higher growth in energy conservation and recycling.

5. TRENDS AND FORCES DIRECTLY AFFECTING OUR SYSTEM

This is where the information and data usually collected for traditional strategic planning is brought into view, the difference being that the group considers the information as a group, rather than as reports analyzed in isolation.

An IT firm's probable future might include items similar to those that emerged in the Motorola search during the mid-1990s:

» expansion and diversification of wireless technology and markets;

» emerging economy economic growth will result in improved living standards and further democratization;
» regional economic alliance will result in a shift in market shares/ manufacturing bases globally;
» wireless technology will evolve – allowing a phone number and communication tool to travel/move with an individual; and
» higher degrees of system-level integration will develop in the personal communication arena.

6. THE SEARCH CONTINUES: DIALOGUE ABOUT "OUR" HISTORY AS AN ORGANIZATION

The purpose of the history dialogue is also to make sure there is a shared knowledge of where the system has come from and all the major formative phases or changes it has gone through, so people are working from the same body of knowledge. This history session is about the organizational system, not about individuals, although individuals are emotionally involved in the history.

Remember your history

A circle is formed with the whole group present. Ask those who are the elders, the veterans of the organization (those who have been with the organization the longest, with the most experience) to speak up first and to tell their view of the company's history. After they begin, others will add their voices. For the next hour or so, the stories people tell bring the group's history to life.

A time-line of formative events emerges. Capture key words on a time-line on flip chart paper. Often, events will seem to be linked with the different leaders over the last decade. The newest people often hear for the first time significant events in their organization's past. Usually it is obvious that the organization's veterans have faced significant obstacles over the past 10 years or so.

Deeply significant learning usually occurs at this point and a sense of the whole is emerging. Telling all the events, their details and relations brings out the total meaning and rich context that lies behind the work the people do. As the time-line approaches the present, more members become involved in putting the story together and a complex web of interdependencies is woven through different experiences.

With both the future of the world and the organization's past contexts in place, you are ready to build upon the history session. There should be sufficient trust in the room now to move into a thorough assessment of the organization's current weaknesses and strengths.

The analysis capitalizes on all the dimensions of the system touched upon by the history session. A purely rational or business analysis loses the subtle cultural factors that give people their unique identity and spirit.

7. THE SEARCH CONTINUES: WHAT TO KEEP, JETTISON, AND CREATE?

As a large group, you explore three questions simultaneously.

» What do we want to keep? For most groups, there is a lot to be proud of.
» What do we want to jettison (throw away)? They will choose to jettison a number of items.
» What do we need to create or invent? This flip chart will often fill quickly.

8. THE SEARCH CONTINUES: CREATING A DESIRABLE GLOBALLY INNOVATIVE FUTURE FOR ACME INC. 2007

In a shifting and uncertain world, a well-defined, desirable future is often expressed in six to eight strategic goals. At the same time, you are working on making your organization as actively adaptive as possible, in relation to achieving those goals and in relation to changes that will occur in the external environment. An active adaptive organization has the ability to align its actions to goals, as well as to modify, drop, or add a particular goal as the environment changes.

Small group work

Form sub-groups to work on creating the desirable future of the operation in 2007. Each group must describe a desirable future in scenarios with no more than seven or eight points. These scenarios may include but are not limited to a definition of market, applications, new technologies, new products, new platforms, organizational structure, business size, etc. The groups work for several hours and then report out their scenarios to the whole group. Disagreement/differences will, of course, surface during this scenario reporting session. Create an agreed and disagreed list using the two following questions to manage this part of the process.

1 Do you have any questions for clarification? As each group presents there are a number of terms and wording that are discussed to avoid confusion and make their meaning plainly evident. Once everyone is clear, you can go on.
2 Is there anything up there in that desirable future of your unit that you could not live with or are not prepared to make happen?

These two questions help rationalize, not resolve, conflict between groups so they can recognize and build common ground. If they failed to ask these questions the groups would focus on what was different in their perspectives rather than what is common or similar. Once such conflict is rationalized, the leadership group is ready and committed to act in concert toward creating an active, adaptive relationship between it and its environment.

Then begin focusing on the areas of agreement – and integrating the work of the sub-groups. Then they produce the goals for the desirable organizational future in 2007 – which are usually a good stretch.

Then look back at the disagreed list to see if any of the items are still relevant to the goals of the agreed-upon desirable future. Any that still remain may be constraints to reaching the desired future. Move those for discussion in the next step.

After integrating the work of four groups, all members should commit to that desirable future and say whether they are prepared to make it happen.

9. ACTION PLANNING TO IDENTIFY GOALS, MEANS TO ATTAIN THE DESIRABLE FUTURE

What are our constraints?

In this session, the group identifies constraints on their desirable future and then develops strategies to overcome those constraints.

Constraints are dealt with close to the end of the search because they are difficult to deal with. Focusing on them before the "community" has experienced itself as confident and creative would be a major obstacle to their progress.

Some typical comments are: "This is hard. It's overwhelming. We want to go home. Can we ever do anything when we've got so much holding us back?" A quick review of the desirable future is usually sufficient to get them moving again.

Brainstorming a list of potential constraints may be the first step. You may also consider using the drivers of innovation mentioned in Chapter 2 as a check list to determine what aspect of a service or product may have been overlooked.

DRIVERS OF INNOVATION CHECK LIST

1 I want to have greater input into the services and products I buy. I want more input into how my community is run, I want great input in my worklife.
2 I want it my way!
3 Low cost and high quality are no longer separate choices.
4 "What's new?"
5 Is it user-friendly?
6 Is it Earth-friendly?
7 Is it people-friendly?
8 Is it beautiful or elegant?
9 Can we trust you?

Another tool that might be used here is to anticipate "unintended consequences," both positive and negative. You may do this by noting on a flip chart the action or decision being made and then ask yourselves, in two or three rounds: "What might happen if we do this?" During each of these rounds, you should try to identify at least two positive and two negative consequences. Each of the potential consequences might then be rated for probability of actually happening using your best estimate – plus or minus 10%, 25%, 50%, or more. The minus or negative ratings will probably indicate that the constraint be dropped from consideration. However, when minus 25% or 50% occurs in a string of otherwise positive consequences, it may simply indicate an area worth looking at for another innovation or breakthrough.

This step takes you several steps into the future and can uncover significant problems as well as unforeseen opportunities. For example, a rip-roaring success may not have considered potential road-blocks in the organization's ability to meet a higher than expected demand for product.

Douglas Aircraft (later McDonnell Douglas) was always a very innovative company, beginning with their DC-3 airplane that revolutionized commercial passenger service. It also had another reputation – it could never quite keep up with orders from airlines around the world for its innovative airplanes. When the airline industry was deregulated in the US, the demand for product substantially increased. Douglas was unable to respond and was taken over by McDonnell. McDonnell could not cure the problem and they eventually merged with Boeing.

Discussing and selecting strategies to overcome constraints

Next, individuals choose one of the top four constraints to work on in small groups. In this new formation, they develop indirect strategies to address that constraint.

Indirect strategies based on *The Art of War* by Sun Tzu, which was compiled over 2000 years ago, are a very effective approach to reaching objectives in a turbulent, uncertain environment. Sun Tzu's strategies do not confront the constraint head on; rather, they encircle, get around, go under, or somehow piggy-back on them to reach our objectives. The following are a few *Art of War* strategies.

1 Concentration as product of diversity:
   » broad-front approach; and
   » not putting all your eggs in the one basket.
2 Effort directed towards points of least resistance and most future potential (multiplier effect). Capture the weakest link.
3 When attacked, pull out. Learning doesn't disappear (good ideas stay in people's heads).
4 Go around and encapsulate the resistance.
5 Encircle from within. Victory and defeat are relative, depending on context. Needs constant re-evaluation of the field while moving

within it. May have to shift effort or sacrifice some efforts, re-assess your priorities.

Lateral thinking, as developed by Edward de Bono (discussed in Chapter 8), might also be used to create means/strategies to overcome constraints.

Because constraints have been put in the positive, groups often find their work here has provided major strategies for moving toward their desirable future.

Now give the group an opportunity to adjust their desirable future in light of all the constraints that have been worked through.

10. ACTION PLANNING, DIFFUSION OF THE PLAN TO THE ORGANIZATION AND IMPLEMENTING THE PLAN

This is the final morning. Participants self-select to participate in self-managing task forces, each of which then develops action plans (strategies and tactics) to achieve their goals. They must agree that no one is leaving until they figure out:

» time parameters for each group;
» criteria for monitoring progress;
» when each group will meet again;
» how they will continue to be self-managing; and
» how to bring other organizational members into the implementation phase.

They accept that they are on their own, fully responsible and that collaboration is now an expected behavior for successful planning.

Rarely in the implementation phase do we deal with a simple linear process.

» There may well be points at which participants realize that additional information is needed and there may be a need to reconvene the original or an enlarged Search Conference community to re-assess priorities and adaptive strategies.
» Sub-groups within a company may want to develop strategies which can fit into the ones developed for the overall business.

» Action plans may require a series of further searches or other methods (such as large group participative events) to involve others throughout the organization.

If and when any of the groups experience such needs or difficulties in carrying out their tasks and strategies, they can now use their experience with the Search Conference method to reconvene as a small group or with the other groups, if necessary, to adjust plans, strategy, or direction.

A FINAL CAUTION

Maintain a self-managing structure. If you should revert to a committee structure with rules of debate, etc., you will have created a mini-bureaucracy with predictable consequences:

» territorial bickering;
» refusal to address primary issues; and
» a rapid decline in attendance, energy, and the enthusiasm you have generated.

A waste of the gains made in the Search Conference.

Frequently Asked Questions (FAQs)

Q1: What is meant by global innovation?

A: See Chapter 2 – The rules of global innovation have changed; there's been an innovation in innovation.

Q2: People are talking about the Global Compact. What is it and what does it have to do with quality?

A: See Chapter 1 – What is the Global Compact and what is its impact on global innovation? and Chapter 2 – The connections between Gandhi, Phil Knight, and the Global Compact.

Q3: What is EDI? What is its role in global innovation?

A: See Chapter 4 – Best practice: EDI at Standard Life.

Q4: What's global about global innovation?

A: See Chapter 5.

Q5: Who has been doing really good work?

A: See Chapter 5 – Best practice case: the Integrated Rural Development (IRD) program in Ireland and Chapter 7 – Australia – Cyclone Hardware P&N Tools.

Q6: Who do I look to for models?

A: See Chapter 6 – Emergent ideas and concepts for the global innovator; and Scouting: the simplest and most effective ongoing innovation tool.

Q7: Where do I go for more information?

A: See Chapter 9.

Q8: Is there a way we can get off to a fast start?

A: Chapter 10 – Ten Steps To Making It Work – Pulling it all Together.

Q9: What about the social and political side of global innovation?

A: See Chapter 6 – Social, political, economic issues; and Web-related issues. See also Chapter 3 – The social and political drivers of global innovation.

Q10: What does the future hold for global innovation?

A: See Chapter 6 – It won't be linear, neat, or predictable; I'm a niche, you're a niche; and I/we want more input into your innovation.

Index

Printed in the United States
By Bookmasters